MALCOLM LOWRY; NOVELIST

Malcolm Lowry Novelist

RAVINDRA PRASAD SINGH

Commonwealth

MALCOLM LOWRY: NOVELIST

Edition 2027

ISBN 81-7169-186-2

Published by :
COMMONWEALTH PUBLISHERS (P) LTD.
4831/24, Govind Lane,
Ansari Road, Darya Ganj,
New Delhi - 110002
Ph. : 23272541, 23242541
e-mail : commonwealthpublishers2016@gmail.com

Distributed by :
ARJUN PUBLISHING HOUSE
4831/24, Govind Lane,
Ansari Road, Darya Ganj,
New Delhi - 110002
Ph. : 23272541, 23242541
e-mail : arjunbooks2001@gmail.com

Laser Typesetting by :
Dimple Computers
Delhi

Printed at :
Milan Enterprises
Delhi

Acknowledgements

I am grateful to S.P. Roy, University Professor of English, B.N. College, Patna University, Patna, under whose able guidance I have completed this study titled "Malcolm Lowry: Novelist". Others to whom I am indebted are Dr. R.K. Sinha, Retired University Professor and Head of the Department of English, Patna University, Dr. R.C. Prasad, University Professor and Head of the Department of English, Patna University and Dr. K.N. Sharma, University Professor of English, P.G. Department, Patna University, Patna. I fail in my duty, if I don't express my gratitude to Muchkund Dubey, a very senior officer in the Indian Foreign Service, who took time off his tight schedule and procured some rare books on Malcolm Lowry for me. For books on Malcolm Lowry I am also obliged to Staff, National Library, Calcutta, the Patna University Library, Patna and The British Council Library, Patna.

RAVINDRA PRASAD SINGH

Contents

Introduction

This critique is an attempt at presenting Malcolm Lowry (1909-1957), an English novelist of our times, with objectivity and detachment. The foremost consideration that has prompted me to write an exegesis of the novels of Malcolm Lowry is to counter misconception about his four published novels—*Ultramarine* (1933), *Under the Volcano* (1947), *Lunar Caustic* (1963) and *October Ferry to Gabriola* (1970). I don't subscribe to this study that his novels are disguised autobiographies. There is no gainsaying the fact that personal element is present in his novels but the presence of personal element is ubiquitious in creative works. A work of art has its genesis in the private emotions of a writer but a good artist strives for developing an impersonal theme out of the matrix of personal experiences. T.S. Eliot's aesthetic assumption that the more perfect the artist, the more completely separate in him will be the man who suffers and the mind which creates, is of paramount importance to all artists and Lowry, perhaps, in keeping with this maxim of T.S. Eliot, works hard to separate the mind from his suffering self, so that enduring works of art are composed.

Ultramarine grows out of Malcolm Lowry's experiences as a deck hand aboard a freighter bound for China but to treat its protagonist Dana Hilliot as a mere replica of the writer is to misread the novel. Through Dana Hilliot Malcolm Lowry tells the story of a rebel against the bourgeois heritage of the family. On a miniature scale he appears to be Joyce's Stephen Dedalus who breaks with home, fatherland and the Church. *Ultramarine*, which is born out of Malcolm Lowry's personal experiences, assumes a universal significance, when it becomes the tale of Everyman bursting with the desire to find a destiny for himself. The existential search of Dana Hilliot, when he affirms in *Ultramarine*: "... it is I who am the father, or who would be the father, the mother and who postulate the responsibility for both..."[1] gives the lie to the reasoning that Lowry's novel is a mere autobiographic projection. *Under the Volcano* has its birth in the private emotion of Malcolm Lowry. Its protagonist Geoffrey Firmin suffers from Lowry's predicament of being in the grip of infernal powers but the novelist presses personal passions hard enough and the predicament of Malcolm Lowry incarnated in Geoffrey Firmin becomes the story of modern man cut off from sanctions, moral and metaphysical. The predicament of the protagonist becomes the predicament of the humanity.

Lunar Caustic and *October Ferry to Gabriola* too develop themes abiding significance out of the personality of the novelist. Bill Plantagenet voices the perennial urge in man to smash the tentacles of guilt by expiation and to establish ties of affection with others, though it is tenuous and fragile. *October Ferry to Gabriola* transcends this world of ours where a character such as Ethan Llewelyn, the hero of the novel, moves out of the maze of self-involvement and reaches after grace numinous in character.

Thus this study I want to submit is that Malcolm Lowry's novels are works of art in their own rights, because Malcolm Lowry all the time exhibits great intelligence and critical instinct in placing and shaping an abundance of material which constantly challenges his organising power. When his critical intelligence fails to shape his personal experiences into a work of art, as he fails in *Dark as the Grave wherein My Friend is Laid*, he runs the risk of being the author of disguised autobiographies. *Dark as the Grave wherein My Friend is Laid* is a diary, an account of Malcolm Lowry's shattering journey through Mexico and it becomes an autobiography and consequently I have not touched upon it in my exposition of his novels.

owry, Malcolm: *Ultramarine*, p. 102.

Malcolm Lowry has also suffered a good deal at the hands of detractors and I presume the antipathy springs perhaps from his being a dipsomaniac. The portrait of Malcolm Lowry is that of a man with a gargantuan appetite for alcohol and a compulsive urge to self-destruction. He is also supposed to be a bundle of neuroses.

A reader not sensitive to the complex organization of a novel such as *Under the Volcano* feels content with identifying the drunkenness of Geoffrey Firmin in the novel with the drunkenness of Malcolm Lowry himself and summarily dismissing the novel as the work of a depraved mind. This palpable misreading of the novel results from our considering it to be a transplant of the personal life of the novelist.

We do justice to Malcolm Lowry, when we abide by D.H. Lawrence's salutary aesthetic principle 'Trust the tale but not the teller'. Malcolm Lowry is writing neither a sociological document on alcoholism nor making a confession of his personal failings. Drunkenness is indeed the theme but the drunkenness of Geoffrey Firmin is symptomatic of the drunkenness of the world as perceived by novelists of the dark night of the soul such as Dostoevsky and Hermann Hesse. Drunkenness in Geoffrey Firmin is planted by the civilization which is out of joint, a civilization which is shot through with jitteriness, a world reeling down the corridors of ruin. The irony is that the apocalypse which is round the corner is the result of his sins of both commission, and particularly, omission.

In this study I make a departure from the conventional assessment of Malcolm Lowry's novels done by the majority of critics who have shifted their attention from the complex interrelations in the organized structure of the novel to the symbolic and mythic interpretation. I am aware of the fact that Malcolm Lowry is not a novelist in the tradition of realists with a sufficient mimetic base. But to wrest symbolic significance out of the total universe of the novel and to ignore completely mimesis is to dehumanize the novel. Malcolm Lowry's novels incarnate their vision in terms of felt experience of life and the emphasis on symbolic and mythic value at the expense of the psychological and literal plane of reality is not a wholesome approach. Mark Schorer's comment on the form of *Under the Volcano* that "it is capable of holding event and symbol, story and meaning absolutely together, of preventing, that is allegory"[1] is an assessment in the right direction.

1. Quoted by Douglas Day in *Malcolm Lowry: A Biography*, p. 381.

1

Malcolm Lowry: A Portrait

Take any brid and put it in a cage
And do al thyn entente and thy corage
To fostre it tenderly with mete and drinke
Of alle deyntees that thou const bithinke
And keep it al-so clenly as thou may
And be his cage of gold never so gay
Yet hath this brid by twenty thousand fold
Lever in a forest that is rude and cold
Gon etc wormes and swich wrecchedness.

—Geoffrey Chaucer, *MauncIples Tale*

Malcolm Lowry was born on July 28,1909 at "Warren-Crest", North Drive, Liscard, in the Birkenhead district of Chesire, England. His father Arthur O Lowry was a wealthy cotton broker and owner of cotton fields in Egypt, Peru and Texas and a director of Sugar and Oil Corporations. His mother Evelyn Boden was the daughter of Captain Lyon Boden, a well known ship owner and mariner. Though Malcolm Lowry was born with a silver spoon in his mouth, he suffered from a sense of emotional abandonment since his boyhood. He recalled to his wife Margerie that his mother had "neglected him terribly".[1] John Davenport, a friend of Lowry at the

1. Quoted in Douglas Day's *Malcolm Lowry: A Biography*, p. 62.

Cambridge, also confirms that Lowry spoke of his mother "only with hatred".[1] Malcolm Lowry had a feeling that he was "the last and least wanted of four children"[2] of Arthur O Lowry.

This sense of alienation that rankles in his mind and finds a manifestation in characters such as Dana Hilliot in *Ultramarine* and Geoffrey Firmin in *Under the Volcano* has become a part of his being since his boyhood. Since his infancy Lowry is left for long periods in the care of nannies, while his mother accompanied her husband on business trips abroad. Lowry once told his wife Margerie that on one occasion a governess had taken him and his brother Russell, aged seven out into a lonely heath near Inglewood, pulled down Lowry's short trousers, and whipped his genitals, while Russell watched. This same woman, he said, later tried to drown him by upending him into a rainbarrel but fortunately he was saved by the gardener. Two months before his death, Lowry told RalphCase, who was visiting him in Ripe that "he had had a nurse in Wirral who used to take him into a remote part of the garden and twist his arm and beat him".[3]

We may take these stories with a grain of salt, but the intensity with which Malcolm Lowry recounts them reveals that the whole episode of the sadistic series of nannies has done an irreparable damage to his being. The psychic dissonance in Malcolm Lowry engendered by sadistic nannies is exacerbated, when at the age of seven he is sent to the boarding-school Caldicote. The spell of separation from parents becomes longer as Malcolm Lowry spends seven long years at Caldicote. His stay at Caldicote is a crucial point in the evolution of his mind. At Caldicote he passes through an ordeal recaptured in the poem Autopsy:

"An autopsy on this childhood reveals
That he was flayed at seven, crucified at eleven

1. *Ibid.*, p. 62.
2. Quoted in Stephen Spender's Introduction to *Under the Biography*, p. XIX.
3. Quoted in Douglas Day's *Malcolm Lowry: A Biography*, p. 66.

And he was blind besides and jeered
For his blindness."[1]

While playing ball at Caldicote, he is struck in the eye and catches infection. The infection remains undiagnosed and for the next four years he remains more than half-blind. It is a galling experience to Lowry that he is left alone in this state of semi-blindness. Malcolm Lowry is shocked to find his mother disgusted at the sight of her youngest son's eyes swathed with heavy bandage. He is seized with consternation when she declines to let him come home. Though his brother Russell refutes that Lowry's infection in the eye goes unattended, it is an undeniable fact that for Lowry himself it is a shattering experience. This episode of blindness is a reality notwithstanding Russell's refutation, because there is scarcely a Lowry protagonist from Dana Hilliot of *Ultramarine* to Ethan of *October Ferry to Gabriola*, who is not shown to have an eye infection during his youth. The loveless treatment Malcolm Lowry receives at the hands of the nursemaid and a prolonged separation from the age of seven to the age of fourteen at Caldicote makes Malcolm Lowry feel forlorn and a castaway and we find him excessively self-engrossed.

James Stern, a novelist and a friend of Malcolm Lowry, speaking of Lowry's extreme self-absorption, says that he has come upon him staring long and broodingly himself at a mirror. Owing to infantile trauma Lowry develops an incapacity to be an extrovert and to contemplate reality as it is in itself and to establish a relation between his own self and the outside world. When this broody and self-absorbed son of Arthur O Lowry. aged fourteen, finishes his schooling at Caldicote, he joins The Leys, Cambridge in September 1923. Even at the Leys Malcolm Lowry feels solitary. One of Lowry's contemporaries at the Leys, W.F. Proudfoot, with fidelity recreates the lonely self of Malcolm Lowry: "I think of Lowry as thick-set in appearance not very tall, tough physically and mentally a little blase and casual in manner, something of a

1. Quoted in M.C. Bredbrook's *Malcolm Lowry*, p. 22.

lonewolf and with a questing mind mature beyond his years. "...I should imagine that much of school life bored him."[1]

He feels out of tune with studies at the Leys and discovers his vocation as a writer. His father wants him to continue his studies at Cambridge but he has other plans. He agrees to go to Cambridge, provided he is allowed to spend a year at sea first. His imagination is fired by Conrad and Eugene O'Neill. Even at the Leys he spins sea yarns to friends and this fascination for sea yarns speaks of a ferment brewing in his imagination. In 1927 he becomes a deckboy on the Pyrrhus bound for Far East. Conrad Knickerbocker writes that the sea voyage before Lowry went to Cambridge "took him to Singapore, Sanghai, Kowloon, Penang (where there was a gun battle in which he was wounded in the leg, glorious young drinking in Yokohama bars, a storm with a dock cargo of snakes, a wild boar, panthers and an elephant."[2]

This sea voyage is not a mere fun. Lowry says, "No silk-cushion youth for me—I want to see the world, and rub shoulders with its oddities, and get some experience of life before I go back to Cambridge University."[3] The son of an affluent cotton merchant embarks on an exploration of what life is like. Some verses from Chaucer's Maunciples Tale prefixed to *Ultramarine* sum up the taste for ordeals that drive Lowry from the parents' ideal of comfort and provision. Like his elder three brothers Stuart, Wilfrid and Russell, he does not want to go into his father's business and lead a life of comfort and ease. He seeks fulfilment in drifting from his family because the seed of alienation from his home, his parents and 'hunting and shooting brothers' is sown in childhood and the seed sprouts and it grows like a sturdy tree. The young Lowry does not fit in with his extrovert three elder brothers. Stuart, the eldest, in fact, once reminisced about what a dreamy and vague little boy Malcolm had been.

This dreamy Malcolm Lowry also feels put out by the strict regimen of an abstemious and puritanical father. Arthur

1. Day, Douglas: *Malcolm Lowry: A Biography*, pp. 79-80.
2. Quoted in Stephen Spender's *Under the Volcano*, p. XXI.
3 Quoted in Douglas Day's *Malcolm Lowry: A Biography*, p. 91.

O Lowry, a Methodist, who saw the pernicious effects of alcohol on some business acquaintance, discouraged drinking at his home, together with smoking, parties and jazz. On the other hand, he put a premium on physical prowess and was a lover of sport. Atop the house where Lowry was born, he built a gymnasium and on his estate at Caldy he laid out a private golf-course. He got an award for saving a drowning man in Mersey. He wanted his sons to follow in his foot-steps, three of them were cast into his mould but the fourth one, that is, Malcolm Lowry, feared the authority of the father. His voyage as a deckboy on the Pyrrhus is motivated by a desire to extricate himself from the fearsome father-figure.

Douglas Day rightly avers that Arthur O Lowry "represented for young Lowry a harsh threatening super ego"[1] of which Freud speaks in Dostoevsky and Parricide. It is not only the super ego embodied in the father that haunts young Malcolm but also the Calvinistic faith of a vengeful God. This idea of a God wreaking vengeance on man certainly unnerves young Malcolm and he wants to get away from such an awesome conception of God.

Malcolm Lowry's voyage by the Pyrrhus (May 1927-October, 27) is impelled by the subterranean impulse in him to sever his relationship with his domineering father Arthur O Lowry whom a biographer of Malcolm Lowry Conrad Kinckerbocker calls, "the incarnation of the imperial middle class."[2] Economically well-off the Lowrys were but the youngest son of Arthur O Lowry finds himself languishing there for want of something that would have nourished the sulking self of young Lowry. In 1929, in his letter to Conrad Aiken, Malcolm Lowry complains that "no body reads at home: the only paper we take is The British Weekly".[3]

This lack of intellectual activity upsets Malcolm Lowry and creates in him a quest for something other than material opulence. On his return from the Asian voyage he goes to English College at Bonn in 1928 (Jan.-March). His stay at

1. Quoted in *Malcolm Lowry: Biography*, p. 64.
2. Quoted in Douglas Day's *Malcolm Lowry: A Biography*, p. 60.
3. *Ibid.*

Bonn also leaves an indelible imprint on his mind. The expressionist German films, dealing with the theme of murder and guilt, considerably affect his imagination and their impact is noticeable in references to expressionist films such as Las Manos de Orlac in *Under the Volcano.* Returning from Bonn he undertakes a journey to New England to spend the summer with Conrad Aiken in 1929. The voyage that takes him to Conrad Aiken is also intimately bound up with the evolution of his mind. Conrad's *Blue Voyage* (published in 1927) had struck the inmost chord of his being and he feels in him an intense desire to write something in the mode of Aiken.

In October, 1929, he goes to Cambridge. At the University he fears the father-figure of his supervisor Tom Henn at Tripos. He picks up friendship with MartinCase at the house of J.B.S. Haldane, an official Bio-Chemistry, and passes a good deal of his time in moving from pub to pub drinking beer and listening to jazz. He also spends a good part of his time writing about his experiences as a deckboy in the freighter Pyrrhus. He is engaged in embodying his experiences as a deckboy in S.S. Pyrrhus in the first novel *Ultramarine.* For Lowry Cambridge University "proved only a return to the cage, much resented."[1] He does not pay much attention to studies in the class room but there is enough evidence to the effect that he has a good collection of books and he perhaps believes in self-schooling.

John Davenport's account of Malcolm Lowry in his study at Cambridge is revealing: "The books revealed the eclecticism of the literary workman. Like other undergraduates of that time he had had a taste for the Elizabethans, Joyce and Eliot, but few undergraduates then knew Knut Hamsun and Herman Bang, B. Traven and Nordahl Grieg. Nor had they read the whole of Ibsen and Strindberg. E.E. Cummings, Hart Crane, Wallace Stevens, and Conrad Aiken himself had merely been names to most of us. Henry James had not been rediscovered, but Malcolm had volume after heavily annotated volume of the Master's work....Three novellas he had an especial affection for were Mann's 'Tonio Kroger', Melville's 'Bartleby'

1. Bradbrook, M.C.: *Malcolm Lowry*, p. 28.

and Bunin's 'The Gentlemen from San Francisco'. Many youngmen of twenty are well read, but Malcolm's reading was integrated in an unusual way. Dante and Faulkner were made to seem part of a whole."[1]

The literary circle at Cambridge is composed of I.A. Richards, Empson, and Jacob Bronowski, Kathleen Raine and Humphrey Jennings, the brilliant film producer. This literary group is interested in Surrealism, Eliot, Joyce and Lawrence. Malcolm Lowry's mind is nourished by the rich intellectual fare at this literary circle. Bronowski's writings on Symbolism and Empson's emphasis on alternative meanings, deep-laid contradictions and paradoxical statement of opposites, must have encouraged Lowry's taste for the multiple levels of meaning and for mythopoeic suspension in his novels later. Among the books prescribed for the Tripos, Baudelaire's '*Fleurs de Mal*' must have tutored his sensibility. Geoffrey's love of damnation in his novel *Under the Volcano* owes much to Baudelaire.

Thus, though Lowry has antipathy to Cambridge, it is an indubitable truth that Cambridge shapes his mind considerably. While at Cambridge he goes to Norway on a freighter in July 1930 to have a meeting with Nordahl Greig. He finds affinity with Nordahl Greig, when he goes through his novel '*The Ship Sails On* (1927).' Thus Malcolm Lowry's stay at Cambridge does a lot to feed his imagination in utter seclusion from his family. At Cambridge he feel that he discovers his identity, when he goes boozing from pub to pub with Martin-Case, J.B.S. Haldane's assistant, or he listens to jazz or participates in a sort of informal salon or open house conducted under the aegis of Haldane's charming young wife Charlotte. But his father Arthur O Lowry becomes alarmed at the spectacular excesses of his son at Cambridge and his intense concern about his determination to pursue a literary career. But mutations already effected in his psyche had gone deep and were now irreversible. He is bent on carving his way in consonance with the promptings of his psyche and after

1. Quoted in Douglas Day's *Malcolm Lowry: A Biography*, p. 112.

getting Class III at English Tripos II at Cambridge, he becomes free of the harsh threatening super-ego of the father.

After Cambridge, Lowry has a London phase during which his novel *Ultramarine* is published. John Sommerfield recalls how Lowry, in the fall of 1932, just drawn from Cambridge "would reel drunkenly about the streets of London, muttering about terrible sexual insults at the hands of nannies which had ruined him for good."[1]

The end of the Cambridge period in Malcolm Lowry's life is a watershed, because his connection with the father is snapped and he begins his long exile in the summer of 1932. He goes to Spain with Conrad Aiken. Malcolm Lowry's lust for wine is so enormous that he startles the Spanish drinkers seated around him. In Spain, a man drank and drank often but he must drink well and Lowry drunk, was anything but dignified. He has an encounter with Jan Gabrial, a 'stunt girl' from Hollywood films in Granada. His marriage with exotic and glamorous Jan Gabrial comes off in Paris. After about six months Jan returns to the States and Malcolm Lowry is in Paris, sharing an apartment with James Stern, a novelist and a story writer. After Paris he goes to New York, he spends ten days in psychiatric wing of Bellevue Hospital, New York. From New York he goes to Hollywood and meets his friend John Davenport and works on several movie scripts. His experience with the cinema is also a grist to the mill of his mind, when he uses cinematic technique such as flash-back, cutting and montage in his novels later.

Along with his wife Jan Gabrial he goes to Mexico, to Cuernavac, which provides the scene of *Under the Volcano*. His marriage with Jan Gabrial breaks down in 1937 and this breakdown of marriage becomes one of the themes in *Under the Volcano*. The Mexican visit stands out in Malcolm Lowry's life, because it gives him a searing experience of life. In 1938, he returns to Hollywood where he meets Margerie Bonner who becomes his second wife.

In 1938, Malcolm Lowry and Margerie move to Vancouver and later to Eastern Canada, near Toronto. Away from the

1. Day, Douglas: *Malcolm Lowry: A Biography*, p. 66.

hellish life of Mexico the Lowrys experience felicity in log cabins and beach-huts built with their own hands. The shack at Dollarton becomes his arcadia and the paradisal experience becomes the stuff of the story *The Forest Path to the Spring*. But misfortune is always at his heels and the local authorities at Dollarton evict Lowry from their beach-hut in early 1950, confiscating the land on which it stood for a public park and burning the cabins to the ground. In sheer disgust the Lowrys decide to leave Dollarton for Italy in September 1954.

While Malcolm Lowry and Margerie are awaiting the departure of a freighter to Italy, he and his wife Margerie stay for two weeks in Professor David Markson's New York apartment. The time spent with Markson is quite amusing and throws ample light on Malcolm Lowry who had made himself an object of mockery on account of his alcoholism. Speaking of Dylan Thomas Lowry told Markson once: "You know, I never saw him when he was not drunk."[1] David Markson wants to begin with the same qualification about Lowry: "The man could not save himself. In lieu of a belt, he knotted a rope or discarded nectie around his waist. Mornings he needed two or three ounces of gin in his orange juice, if he was to steady his hand to eat the breakfast that would, very likely prove his only meal of the day. Thereafter, a diminishing yellow tint in the glass might belie for a time the fact that now he was drinking the gin neat, which he did for as many hours as it took him to collapse sometimes sensible enough of his condition to lurch toward a bed, though more often he would crash down into a chair, and once it was across my phonograph. Then he would hack and sputter through the night like some great defective machine breaking apart."[2]

David Markson also relates that one afternoon in New York they leave Malcolm Lowry alone for a time within the apartment. They hide gin and leave him with six or eight cans of beer. When they return, they find to their utter dismay that Lowry has drunk a fresh bottle of shaving lotion.

1. Markson David: *The Nation*, Feb. 7, 1966, p. 164.
2. *Ibid.*, p. 164.

Bul this is not a complete picture of the man. Conard Aiken's account in *Ushant* is a powerful tribute to the young author's conquering charm: "That most engaging and volatile and unpredictable of geniuses; for surely of all the literary folk... there had been none among them who had been so visibly or happily alight with genius—not that the TseTse (T.S. Eliot) hadn't manifested something of the same thing to be sure—controlling it moreover to better purpose—but in Hambo (Lowry) it had been the more moving, and convincing, and alive, for its very uncontrolledness, its spontaneity and gay recklessness, not to mention its infectious gleeful delight in itself... life itself was a picnic of genius in which every one could share."[1]

Thus the "most engaging and volatile and unpredictable of geniuses" with a sojourn in Italy reaches Ripe, a village in Sussex, and dies there on June 1957. He is made up of two contradictory impulses—a kind of naivete and a winsome infectious joy and a demonic glitter in his Scandinavian eyes, with the upper teeth protruding slightly, suggestive of a grin whether one was intended or not, making of him roguishly improbable Faustus at best. He swings between the two extremes of despair and elation.

The duality in Malcolm Lowry brings him closer to Blake's metaphysic summed up in *Marriage of Heaven and Hell*: "without Contraries is no progression. Attraction and Repulsion, Reason and Energy, Love and Hate, are necessary to Human existence."[2] The contrary states of soul inhering in the opposed impulses of love and hate are enacted in his novels from *Ultramarine* to *October Ferry* to *Gabriola*. Molcolm Lowry wrings powerful poetry out of the dialectics of love and hate.

1. Bradbrook, M.C.: *Malcolm Lowry*, p. 20.
2. Blake, William: *The Marriage of Heaven and Hell*, p. 123.

2

Ultramarine

> His soul had arisen from the grave of boyhood spurning her grave-clothes. Yes! Yes! Yes! He would create proudly out of the freedom and power of his soul, as the great artificer whose name he bore, a living thing, new and soaring and beautiful, impalpable, imperishable.
>
> —James Joyce, *A Portrait of the Artist*

(A) DOMINANT THEMES

Dana Hilliot is the nucleus round which Malcolm Lowry's first novel *Ultramarine* (1933) revolves. Dana Hilliot becomes a member of the crew on the deck of the ship Oedipus Tyrannus bound for the Far East. He becomes a sailor for the sake of fun and when the Quarter Master wants to know from Hilliot about the motive that prompted him to become a sea-man he tells him that he has chosen seamanship not as a calling or vocation but for the sake of sheer enjoyment of life. Hilliot's choice of a ship as a vehicle for the enjoyment of life is quite significant. When he boards the ship, he finds an affinity with it. He has kinship with the ship in the sense that both are without an identity of their own. In Chapter Two in his soliloquy within parenthesis he introduces the Oedipus Tyrannus to his girl friend Janet. He says:

> "Both of us born of Viking blood, both robbed of our countries and left to make out as best we can; both, finally,

> with the same wandering, harbourless, dispossessed characteristics."[1]

Hilliot says that the history of the ship fills him with a narcissistic compassion for it. He traces the history of the Oedipus Tyrannus: "First she was registered in Tvedestrand, then bought by an English firm, who re-registered her, altering her derrick plan, then she was bought back by Norway; after which she was rebought by England and, after her reconditioning was completed, received a charter."[2] This frequent change of nationalities in respect of the ownership of the steamer robs it of a separate identity and makes it a cosmopolitan one. At one place in the novel the writer calls it, 'Whoreship' suggestive of a slippery woman devoid of fidelity in marital life.

Dana Hilliot's history of life resembles that of Oedipus Tyrannus. Varied cultures have gone into his making. Like the Oedipus Tyrannus he too is wandering harbourless and dispossessed. Before he is five he is taken away on interminable voyages all over the world. He nurses a grudge against life that he fails to strike roots into the soil of a particular land. The to and fro movement from one country to the other does an irreparable damage to him. Speaking of the anguish of spirit resulting from his roving from one country to the other he says "...every country from which I have been forced to emigrate has left a gaping hole in my heart, considering the fomenting heterogeneity of the crew, the minute Greek and Spanish and French firmament as well as the Norse, English and American—is it any wonder that I feel humiliated by it all, and as homeless, as exiled as the ship itself ?"[3]

The wandering Jew in Eliot's *Gerontion* does not belong to a particular culture. He is "spawned in some estaminet of

1. Lowry, Malcolm: *Ultramarine*, (Jonathan Cape, Thirty Bedford Square, London, 1969), p. 53.
2. *Ibid.*, p. 53.
3. *Ibid.*, pp. 53-4.

Antwerp/Blistered in Brussels, patched and peeled in London."[1] Hilliot has had his brief education in Oslo, thereafter he has an affair with Janet and when his father receives a tutorial assignment at Harvard, he finds himself uprooted from his native land.

The elaborate comparison Hilliot makes of his life with that of the ship shows that Hilliott becomes a sailor not out of mere fun but out of a deep turmoil in his psyche. The commotion in Hilliot has been engendered by his movement from one country to the other since his boyhood. He wants to cling to a stable point in his ever-wandering life. Behind the facade of fun and enjoyment lurks the smouldering fire of profound unrest. Hilliot's reply to the Quarter Master that he joins the ship out of fun is not to be taken at its face value. Behind this stock and glib reply lies the wounded sensibility of Hilliot. His fascination for the ship may partly be attributed to the teeming chaos of the sea very much similar to his chaotic mental state.

Hilliot suffers from a basic flaw in his life. He lacks order and harmony since his school days. As a student of Euclid's geometry he cuts a very poor figure in the class and receives a reprimand from the mathematics teacher. He becomes a butt of ridicule, when his classmates crowd around him to watch his pathetic attempt to create a regular hexagon. At school geometry puzzles and frightens Hilliot and it eventually becomes a sort of monster to him. This inability of Hilliot to draw geometrical figures with exactness and precision is symptomatic of a deeper chaos in his life. In Chapter I the novelist tells us about this fundamental incapacity of Hilliot: "For here as nowhere else he could understand precisely what was so all-poisoning in him, this incapacity to position things and see them their places."[2]

This inability to see things as they are in themselves and to see them in the right perspective is not a predicament of Hilliot only, but a dilemma gnawing at the heart of every modern, especially people of the thirties. T.S. Eliot's *Gerontion*

1. Eliot, T.S.: *Selected Poems*, (Faber & Faber Limited), p. 31.
2. Lowry, Malcolm: *Ultramarine*, p. 40.

suffers from such a predicament when says: "I was neither at the hot gates/ Nor fought in the warm rain/ Nor knee deep in the salt marsh, heaving a cutlass."[1] The civilization has become a heap of broken images and values are in a state of disarray. Hilliot voices the anguish of the humanity of his time. The chaotic state of civilization is discernible, when Hilliot goes to a big hall where he see an old harridan with a saggy face, evidently a European, shuffling in carpet slippers. Around the room meant for fleshpots and sensual enjoyment are Biblical mottoes and the prints of Virgin Mary and Mary Magdalene. He also finds a large bed with much-haloed Jesus above it intruding on his consciousness and next to Jesus, a meek kitten.

The harridan invites Hilliot to immerse himself in the enjoyment of delights of the flesh but Hilliot is circumscribed by the promise he had made to Janet before embarking on a voyage to Far East. Hilliot suffers from a conflict. On the one hand, his commitment to Janet that he will keep himself undefiled throughout the voyage rings in his ears and on the other, the sensual delights dangle before him a world of delectable romance and entice Hilliot by offering the prospect of dalliance. The voyage is a objective correlative for voyage through the psyche of Hilliot from the state of purity into damnation.

Hilliot, who is considered to be the alter ego of Malcolm Lowry, is obsessed with self-destruction. The memory of Janet is a phase in Hilliot's consciousness characterised by purity and virginity and the moment he takes leave of Janet and boards the ship, he finds himself face to face with evil and all through voyage we find Hilliot wrestling with evil. When he steps ashore he finds a small anatomical museum. In this museum he sees the aweful effects of "Man leading a DEPRAVED life visiting the iniquity of FATHERS upon the CHILDREN and upon the CHILDREN'S children unto the third and fourth GENERATION..."[2] He reads the stern Biblical injunction that when men disobey the laws of

1. Eliot, T.S.: *Selected Poems*, p. 31.
2. Lowry, Malcolm: *Ultramarine*, p. 110.

God, they suffer the inevitable consequence of death. The Biblical maxim "... if any man defile the temple of God, him will God destroy. for the temple of God is holy,..."[1] and it contrasts with the fleshpots and sensual enjoyment.

It has been argued by a host of reviewers that traces of imitativeness are palpable in *Ultramarine*. They feel that Lowry is a plagiarist stealing from Conrad Aiken's *Blue Voyage* and Nordahl Grieg's *The Ship Sails On*. There is no denying the fact thet Lowry read Conrad Aiken and Nordahl Grieg, when he was engaged in the writing of *Ultramarine* but it will be a distortion of fact, if *Ultramarine* is considered to be a work of pastiche incorporating the themes of *Blue Voyage* and *The Ship Sails On*. The affinity with Conrad Aiken and Nordahl Grieg is not confined to influences obviously discernible in *Ultramarine*. The affinity goes deep and is related to the mode of perceiving the reality.

Lowry's obsession is with the taint that has blighted human soul. The evil proliferates and envelops all and eats away their vitals. In Chapter Third the protagonist, Dana Hilliot, who projects the predicament of the author himself, tells us about the days of his boyhood, since when his obsession with guilt torments him. In Chapter Three, he talks about himself gazing at the picture of his grandfather in old nursery. The infinitely blue eyes of the grandfather were a reproach to him "why are you so dirty, Dana."[2] The grandfather was always so clean, so spruce that he appeared to be an 'angel from heaven.'[3] But he had sunk into the inferno of evil passions and when he would return from his voyage. he would find himself a fallen creature quite unbecoming of his beloved Janet.

Conrad Aiken and Nordahl Grieg were also concerned with the exploration of vile passions making a wreck of human life. They chose the medium of the sea for the exploration of man's encounter with evil that slumbers in his soul. It is the elemental simplicity of the sea that becomes a

1. *Ibid.*, p. 111.
2. *Ibid.*, p. 118.
3. *Ibid.*, p. 119.

fit vehicle for laying bare the havoc the fury of wild passions plays with man. Lowry's likeness with Conrad Aiken and Nordahl Greig is on the score of the sea becoming a medium of projecting the self-destructive vision of the writer.

The sea was in his blood. It was so partly owing to his going through the works of O'Neill, Conrad Aiken and Nordahl Greig and partly to his nearness to Caldy and Chesire in the vicinity of the port of Liverpool. The configuration of Wirral Peninsula with its sinister and awesome landscape inhabited by pirates, who rob those who escape the perils of the sea and come safe to the shore, breeds toughness in him.

Though Hilliot, the alter ego of Lowry, is preoccupied with low passions corrupting him, he searches for some absolutes of life. He says, "If we will ever find it, Absolute beauty, absolute truth, did they exist?"[1] His search for a stable point in life is marred by his scepticism. The predominant impression his voyage aboard the Oedipus Tyrannus leaves on the reader is that of utter ruin and chaos as the first principle of life. Hilliot says, "Chaos and disunion, then, he told himself, not law and order, were the principles of life which sustained all things, in the mind of men as well as on the ship."[2] The furnace of the ship vividly described is a veritable hell where firemen are like demons. With great fascination Hilliot watches a fireman Nikolai half-naked, gritty and black with coal and pasty with ashes and blazing light and gloom. Hilliot's search for absolute truth and beauty gets bogged down in the slough and mire of vile passions to which he finds himself susceptible.

He gives a lurid and macabre account of himself in course of his talk with a German sailor in Chapter III of the novel. He considers himself to be queer, because of the incredible things he does. His youth is ruined by curious passions for collecting among other things, universities. He plays baseball in Harvard and sets fire to Brattle Square. He moves to Princeton where he nearly drinks himself to death. In Moscow

1. *Ibid.*, p. 119.
2. *Ibid.*, p. 169.

he becomes a cameraman and at Cape Cod he holds office simultaneously as the town constable, the ticket collector at the cinema and the local bootlegger and it is there he commits his first murder in a windmill. In Barbados, in Bridgetown he remains a week playing the taropatch in a brothel. While accepting the offer of the fifteeen-year-old daughter of the house, he sells her to the Negro door-keeper for a bottle of gin. In Stamboul he plays chess with Sultan's sister.

He pursues women from street to street, from land to land, always remaining a virgin. When they speak to him, he runs away. All his acts and behaviour bear testimony to the fact that he is really a strange character. But to take Hilliot's words prima facie that he is merely a strange character will be reading the novel not in the right perspective. He appears to be a strange character to his mother and to his beloved Janet. The mother is preoccupied with the purity and integrity of the character of her son. The letter Hilliot receives from the mother in course of his voyage on the deck of the Oedipus Tyrannus has the central theme: "I don't want my son to be coarsened by a set of hooligans."[1]

Hilliot keeps the letter of his mother in his pocket and when he meets the German sailor Pcpplereuter, he hands over the letter to him and asks him to read it out to him. The letter contains the holy injunction "I do not want my son to be coarsened by a set of hooligans." The words of the mother sound to him as pious protestations of a mother's solicitude for the physical and moral well-being of the son. They sound cliches to him and the journey through different harbours comes to Hilliot in all its myriad forms of the reality of the mundane world. The moral maxim of the mother is too fragile to cope with the multitudinous spectacle of life offering formidable challenges and is sullied by Hilliot's desire for the banquet of sense.

The novelist through Hilliot's voyage on the deck of the Oedipus Tyrannus wants to present the gradually unfolding

1. *Ibid.*, p. 124.

kaleidoscopic view of life. At the beginning of Chapter III Hilliot says, "I would have to find all that out for myself."[1] When he first comes to the ship, he is treated as an alien, a toff, and all took askance at him. The cook Andy becomes a source of nuisance to him and he is always itching for a row with Hilliot. As Benjamin Hall of Nordahl Grieg's *The Ship Sails On* is haunted by the supposed guilt that he has murdered Anton, he, too, suffers from the inexplicable feeling of having caused injury to Andy.

The ship is a community, a cosmos, a world based on the principle of hierarchy and Hilliot is an intruder into that community of sailors. The sense of alienation from that community initially rankles in his mind but it wears off and Hilliot acclimatizes himself to the moral and spiritual clime of the sea towards the end of the novel. He becomes one of them and heaves a sigh of relief on his acceptance by the community. He had misconceptions that the sea would be opening up the vista of interminable beauty but he found that that was not the way of things. He had to suffer the ordeal of arduous labour, when his right arm ached terribly with sea boils. In place of the open sea, the wind racing through the blood and stars twinkling in the firmament, he saw gritty coal dust everywhere and the swarm of flies heaved and sizzled and bred on the bulkheads. Coal dust got in his eyes and blackened his nostrils and he could not stand the heavy smell.

The ship is a miniature universe and Hilliot finds himself descending from the level of simplicity and purity into the realm of multiplicity and vileness. When he looks more deeply into the glass containing gin, he finds reflected therein sadness, misery, self-disgust, terror. Journey by the Oedipus Tyrannus does not mean that he is getting away from the reality that unnerves a man: "No getting away from it, no getting away from the unfortunate Hilliot, this strong creature with a head of filthy, infected hair, and a maggoty and rotting consciousness who dreams of archetypal images."[2]

1. *Ibid.*, p. 79.
2. *Ibid* , p. 98.

He considers the voyage to be a 'self-inflicted penance'. He undertakes journey by sea in order to make an exploration of what life is like and this exploratory nature of the voyage entails immense suffering for him. He believes that the ultimate reality is experienced only after passing through a phase of ordeal. Hilliot is not only a voyager coursing through the harbours of several oriental lands. He often proclaims the intention of becoming a writer. As a writer he wants to grapple with the essentials of life, and among writers he is under the spell of Joseph Conrad who gives us the harrowing tale of a civilized and sophisticated European Mistah Kurtz through the Congo. The mantle of learning and civilization falls off Mistah Kurtz and he comes before the reader as a brute in the midst of African savages. The darknesss of Africa reclaims his soul and Kurtz sinks to the level of wild animals governed by inordinate lust for ivory, though his despairing utterance 'The horror! The horror!'[1] faintly redeems him.

Lowry's Hilliot is not a Mistah Kurtz but the affinity with Kurtz is there because both are educated and civilized people and embark on a voyage and find themselves face to face with stark realities that come to the fore ripping open the veneer of propriety and decorum. The excerpt from Chaucer's Maunciples Tale that acts as a prologue to *Ultramarine* gives the reader an intimation of its protagonist's subterranean impluse to filth and slime. The bird gorging on all dainties in a cage of gold feels a captive and comes out of it and embraces the 'rude and cold'[2] forest and feeds on worms. Russell Lowry, an elder brother of Malcolm Lowry, knows him from the inside when he observes: "He was more interested in slime than in silk, in stinks rather than mere smells, in the sordid rather than the sublime. The boiling muck under his volcano was more appealing to him than the snow on its summit."[3] Though Hilliot sees the anatomical museum depicting the depravity and iniquity of people with

1. Conrad Joseph: *Heart of Darkness* (The New American Library, 1959), p. 133.
2. Lowry, Malcolm: *Ultramarine*, p. 11.
3. Edited by Anne Smith: *The Art of Malcolm Lowry*, p. 27.

the solemn injunction that 'The wages of sin is death', he does not suffer from the qualms of conscience entering the brothel and having an affair with the Russian strumpet Olga Sologub. He does not heed the warning that any indulgence in sensual passions invites the wrath of God and he wantonly falls into the pit of sensuality. After having had the enjoyment of drinking bouts and of pursuing women after women, he sometimes feels that he is treading in a ruinous path.

He wants to have peace and harmony in place of strife and turmoil and his yearning for peace and harmony finds a positive expression in his attempt to save Norman's mickey that was drowned in the sea. Andy prevents him from leaping into the sea water in order to salvage the drowned mickey of Norman, because the sea is infested with sharks and crocodiles. He yields to the arguments of Andy and refrains from jumping into the sea. However, the idea to salvage the drowned mickey is a movement towards something creative in the life of a character who is prone to despondency and cynicism. The movement towards peace and harmony in Hilliot's mind is not something smug and is not forced on him, but it grows out of his experience with the complex maelstrom of life. Harmony, of which Hilliot speaks, emerges from disharmony and chaos of life. He rightly avers: "Why was it his brain could not accept the dissonance as simply as harmony, could not make order emerge from this chaos. Surely God had made men free from the first, tossing confusion of slime, the spewings of that chaos, from the region beast. Chaos and disunion, then, he told himself, not law and order, were the principles of life which sustained all things, in the mind of men as well as on the ship."[1]

Hilliot's reconciliation with Andy is another proof of growing self-knowledge in Hilliot. From the very beginning of the voyage on the Oedipus Tyrannus Andy appears to Hilliot as a red rag to a bull. Andy rouses his ire and Hilliot nurses a grudge against Andy. He cannot get over his sense

1. *Ibid.*, p. 169.

of wonder mingled with hate at the sight of chinless Andy. But towards the end of the journey he finds himself in such situations with Andy that his unreasoning hatred of Andy gives way to his love for him. This relationship is the result of sympathetic understanding in Hilliot that enables him to peel off misconceptions about man and reality. Till a long part of the voyage he finds himself a toff and an outsider but realisation dawns on him, when the compulsive events of life make demands on him smashing his illusory ideas.

Hilliot's experiences as an ordinary seaman on the deck of the Oedipus Tyrannus fall into two distinct groups—first his experience of detestation not of himself but of the crew and secondly the realisation that the act of despising others is not a healthy attitude, because it breeds bitterness and ruin. The unrelenting hatred in him towards Andy passes into goodwill and love for him, because he suffers from remorse for nursing a grudge against Andy and other members of the crew. The impulse to despise was so overwhelming in him that he invented an abominable tale about his parents. In a disrespectful vein he speaks of his father and mother: "Like myself, like Herman Bang, like the ship, like my excellent father, the only surviving son, who is now in a home eating the buttons off the chair...and composing a sonnet sequence. Song of Second Childhood...While my mother who occasionally writes me is going blind."[1]

He too is contemptuous of himself, when he says how everyone, Dana Hilliot, the syphilitic, touches is smitten with the dire disease and he gives way to complete despair with the realization that he is the human husk, the leaf of ash, ashes to ashes and dust to dust. But towards the end of the novel we find Hilliot assuming a role just the reverse of that of cynician and ruin. In one of his epistles to Janet at the end of the novel he weaves a tale altogether different, when he has learnt to live with the unpalatable reality of the hard facts of life, viewing those facts from the angle of 'sanity and detachment'.

1. *Ibid.*, p. 72.

He is no longer weary of the journey by the Oedipus Tyrannus, because he learns how to take things in his stride. He overcomes the sense of being an alien on the deck of the ship. When he first steps into the ship, he acutely suffers from the pangs of separation from Janet. The misery of parting is unbearable and the loving memories of Janet haunt his mind in course of the journey. The irksome feeling that Janet is away from him is exacerbated by the misery in adjusting himself to the ship conjoined with the misery of his all-consuming envy of Andy.

On top of all these painful facts is the excruciating frustration he experiences one afternoon. But from this frustration, the worst in his life, issues the greatest good of his life. In this mood of anguish tearing apart his very being he tells Andy of his love for Janet. Andy reveals to him a truth about the very business of love-making by stripping off romantic illusion hanging about love. He loses many illusions and has a perfectly clear vision of himself. He becomes one with Andy with all his frailties. The component parts of Andy "...the fulsome fleshpots and the woman-scented evenings, the rough red drawers and the bawd and lodging"[1] become his mental wardrobe.

This he calls identification with Andy and is symbolic of his being soaked in the palpable facts of life. "Howsoever unedifying", he says, "I have to accept Andy and that is no more dangerous than accepting life".[2] Andy's vision is clear. He does not suffer from any ostrich-like complacency. He stares reality in the face and there is nothing squeamish about his character. He has been steeled into granite-like firmness who is not put out in the least by the gritty reality. Hilliot says that his will be the lot of journeying through "a land corrupted and depressed beyond all knowledge, where the children are starving for lack of milk",[3] a land unhappy, and with radiant energy he will cope with this cheerless and nerve-racking land. Instead of fathoming the shallows, he would

1. *Ibid.*, p. 186.
2. *Ibid.*, p. 186.
3. *Ibid.*, p. 186.

whip the sea or deface his mother's house. He makes this snatch a governing principle of his life: "But grieving's a folly,/Come, let us be jolly/I we've troubles at sea, boys, we've pleasures ashore."[1]

Hilliot is now not interested in pleasures ashore but he has girded up his loins and considers grieving to be a folly. He will wrestle with reality. At the end of the novel he conjures up a vision of a journey bouncing with life towards the burning seas of light. Disease, sickness, cynicism and despair fall away and Hilliot is seen moving "...towards the summer, towards those burning seas of light; to sit at night in the forecastle lost in an unfamiliar dream, when the spirit becomes filled with stars, instead of wounds, and good and compassionate and tender. To sail into an unknown spring, or receive one's baptism on storm's promontory, where the solitary albatross heels over in the gale, and at last come to land...All around is the desert save where a cluster of palms struggle in the noonday fire; the eternal stream, which once was lost but lived always in the dream of man".[2]

This paragraph brings to the fore an aspect of Malcolm Lowry that redeems him from writing a tale of gloom and cynicism in *Ultramarine*. It is the aspect of creativity that masters disharmony and cacophony and imposes a meaningful order on the welter of facts that tend to sap his grip on life. In the concluding chapter of the novel his love for Janet has the universal experience of sublimated all-embracing love for mankind. This all-encompassing love for mankind becomes Hilliot's quest towards the end of the novel.

The novel becomes an affirmation of life as the protagonist finds himself gliding slowly through the "grey, sun-bleached land where the desert men kneel in still, confident peace, where the darkness draws in a moment. Where the wild mysteries of the desert nights gleam in everything, in the sand garden's waste, in the palm's breath, in the starlight's cold, and in stars in motion on the dark stream."[3] Hilliot resolves to fight

1. *Ibid.*, p. 177.
2. *Ibid.*, p. 201.
3. *Ibid.*, p. 201.

always for the dreamt-of-harbour, when the sea thunders on board in a cataract, and the ship rolls and wallows in the track of the frozen sea's storm.

This resolution of Hilliot to go ahead in the teeth of darkness closing in on him gives a lie to critics who brand him as a writer sold to infernal powers of darkness. Darkness is within human mind like the elements of goodness. Lowry is not a smug moralist who glosses over darkness and raw components of man. He finds himself in the thick of the powers of darkness and confidently wades through inferno catching a glimpse of the creative principle of love, though his hold on it is not very firm.

Despite the fact that his grasp of the reality of love is tenuous, its presence is ubiquitous. Malcolm Bradbury in his essay on Malcolm Lowry rightly points out that in Lowry there is a "sense of love as a transcendent principle and an upward movement, through which things have greater distinctiveness and separateness".[1] Lowry saw it as a moral force, the supernatural world informing the material. Even *Under the Volcano* in which Geoffrey Firmin makes a destructive identification, love affirms itself from the start to the finish. George Firmin who resembles Marlowe's Doctor Faustus selling his soul to powers of darkness, is acutely aware of love as a saviour: "How could he have thought so evil of the world when succour was at hand all the time? And now he had reached the summit. Ah! Yvonne, sweetheart, forgive me."[2]

(B) ART OF CHARACTERISATION

It has been said about Malcolm Lowry that he has a solipsistic vision of life and he creates characters as a projection of his own mind. Characters do not have an independent entity, because they represent the different facets of the personality of the novelist himself. But this point of view does not hold good, when we take into account Lowry's art of characterisation in *Ultramarine*. We can divide characters into three

1. Bradbury, Malcolm: *Possibilities*, (Oxford University Press), p. 199.
2. Lowry, Malcolm: *Under the Volcano*, p. 375.

categories—the first category is constituted of the protagonist Dana Hilliot, the second category is that of Dana Hilliot's parents and his beloved Janet and the third group is a curious assortment of characters ranging from the crew to characters like Hans Popplereuter and a Russian refugee prostitute Olga Sologub. Of the crew many are called by the designations of their calling. Only two of the crew Norman and Andy, instead of being shadowy, are developed in terms of telling details. It is not only human characters that matter in the novel.

The ship that moves from one port to another with the character of a whore is of no less significance, because the ship is the catalyst that sets off changes of far-reaching significance in the protagonist. Lowry takes pains to delineate with great fidelity and delicacy the ship that throbs with life and he finds himself one with the ship. The theme of the novel emerges from this interaction of Dana Hilliot, his beloved Janet's ubiquitous presence as a guardian angel and his mother's injunction to keep inviolate his purity, the antipathy of Andy, the cook and the ship as a replica of Dana Hilliot.

Dana Hilliot, a youngman of nineteen, is born in Oslo. From the age of five he has been on an interminable voyage all over the world. From Oslo he goes to Harvard where his father gets a tutorial assignmnent. Strolling with his father through the Harvard Yard passing the Widener Library he has had a nice time. He says, "How gay we were, happy enough then with our sausage and buckwheat and root beer: With our oysters and swordfish and quahaug and clams; and the hermit crab, that pirate of crabs, seeking its shelly cave...".[1] This life gaiety and sensuous enjoyment contrasts with the painful memory of "...a rotten time in Oslo. Nothing but working as hell, a lot of us in stuffy rooms."[2]

From Harvard he comes to Oxford on scholarship for one year. Of Oxford he says: "That was very funny. It was nothing but 'have another gin' all the time, balancing tea cups and talking; my God, you know how damnable it is."[3] He

1. Lowry, Malcolm: *Ultramarine*, p. 54.
2. *Ibid.*, p. 54.
3. *Ibid.*, p. 54.

moves over to Cambridge in quest of wonderful friendships, freedom, youth...He indulges himself in booz racket in Cambridge. He does not get along with people at Cambridge. In a'mood of sheer disgust and weariness he gives account of his one year stay at Cambridge: "It was nothing, nothing at all. I failed my first-year examinations, Verstehn Sie, what we call 'Mays'. And I was had up once for leaving a pub after ten—what you call a Weinlust. And I was arrested on November fifth for knocking off a policeman's hat. Silly, silly, silly things. The Master of the College sent for me and said, "You neither ride, row nor read—"[1]

This unseemly and disappointing performance of Hilliot's at Cambridge upsets his guardian who says to him—"You better settle down now and do some work."[2] This is perhaps reminiscent of Lowry himself whose spectacular excesses at Cambridge prompt his father Arthur O Lowry to come over from Liverpool to London to set his son straight. Douglas gives an account of Lowry's aberrations and his father's anxiety for the well being of the son: "Mr. Lowry somehow found time during the afternoon to confide to Aiken that he was very concerned about his son: Not only did Malcolm seem determined to pursue a literary career—which was bad enough—but he had recently found an obscene letter from a friend at St. Catherine's in Malcolm's dresser drawer, and feared that his son was on his way to a life of real depravity."[3]

But if we say that the portrait of Dana Hilliot is an autobiographical snatch, it is nothing but to ignore the art of the novelist that gives a shape to the turmoil brewing in the mind of the novelist himself as well as in the mind of the protagonist. Margerie Lowry in Introduction to *Ultramarine* rightly says, "The most important thing about this book, to me, is not its partially autobiographical content, but the fact that at this early period Malcolm was already so completely the self-conscious artist, in the control of his material and his

1. *Ibid.*, p. 95.
2. *Ibid.*, p. 95.
3. Day, Douglas: *Malcolm Lowry* (A Biography, 1974), p. 120.

style."[1] Thus Dana Hilliot, no doubt, reveals the conflict raging in the mind of the novelist but over and above this, he is a youngman who feels put out by the snub of authorities at Cambridge that he is not fit for education imparted there and the affront is exacerbated by the court and peremptory words of the guardian that he should settle down to some work.

The trouble that fills him with disquiet has its root in his vacillation. From the very outset of the novel he wavers from one thing to the other, because he cannot understand precisely what is at the root of his unease. The incapacity to position things and see them in their places gnaws at his heart. He falls an easy prey to despair: "How easy, how desperately easy, it would be to put an end to everything. A sudden impetus of mind, the relaxing of a muscle, and it would all be over. He seated himself on one of the top rungs...Buried at sea."[2]

These cynical reflections haunt him, when he becomes a deckboy on the Oedipus Tyrannus bound for the Far East. He takes to voyage goaded partly by the chilly words of guardian that he should settle to some work and partly by his search for identity in the vein of Eugene O'Neill's Yank in *The Hairy Ape*. The latter urge is imperious all the more, because Dana Hilliot feels that like the Oedipus Tyrannus he too is bereft of a determined character. It is not unlike Sartre's world in *Nausea* where Roquentin says that the essential thing is contingency, where no necessary or stable relationships are to be discerned, which is sensed primarily as a viscuous flux.

Though Dana Hilliot feels akin to the ship, the ship does not turn out to be hospitable to him. First, it seemed to Hilliot that the Oedipus Tyrannus had a manifold security: "She was his harbour, he would lie in the arms of the ship, the derricks would fold about him like wings, sleep would bring with it a tender dream of home, of Suns and fields and barns."[3] But the dream of a cosy hearth remains a mirage.

1. Lowry, Malcolm: *Ultramarine*, p. 7.
2. *Ibid.*, p. 40.
3. *Ibid.*, p. 43.

Dana Hilliot's dream of a smooth voyage meets with a stiff resistance from the crew, especially Andy, with enormous arms and an acutely weak chin supplemented with a dignified forehead. Andy is a thirtynine-year-old Norwegian cook, tattooed all over; a Norwegian flag, a barque in full sail, a heart, presumably, and God knows what. He has spent twenty long years voyaging all over the world. But Dana Hilliot is on a maiden voyage. Andy is unsympathetic and morose at the sight of Dana Hilliot, because he looks upon him as an outsider, with no nexus with the clime of the Oedipus Tyrannus. Andy's constant refrain about Dana Hilliot is: "We do not know what sort of bloody man you are at all."[1] Andy takes delight in heaping ignominy and calumny on Dana Hilliot, calling him a nancy, an effeminate seaman. In a vein of mockery he calls him Miss Hilliot. "Hurry up there, Miss Hilliot, seven bells gone half an hour ago, your lady ship."[2]

It is nerve-racking for Hilliot to become a butt of ridicule amongst shipmates, when with great fervour he has become a deckboy on the Oedipus Tyrannus. Andy's antipathy has a chilling effect on Hilliot. "I suppose you think it's pretty good coming to sea. Well, you'll find out pretty soon what it's like; it's just a question of working as hell—one port's the same or another. Yes, you'll find out pretty soon."[3] Andy's detestation gets on his nerves and he strives after something that will redeem him in this predicament of appalling isolation from the community of the Oedipus Tyrannus.

An opportunity comes to him, when he can show to his shipmates that he is not alien to their community, rather he belongs to them. A carrier pigeon from Swansea that had perched on the tapering mainmast commands his attention. Hilliot wants to impress the shipmates with his heroic exploits when he tells them that he is willing to undertake the perilous climb of the mainmast in order to save the mickey. All laugh at his audacity. They treat his gesture as the swagger of a

1. *Ibid.*, p. 16.
2. *Ibid.*, p. 21.
3. *Ibid*, p. 19.

swelled-head and not an act of compassion. He recoils from contemplated adventure of rescuing the dunghawk and Norman a twenty-nine year old Norwegian galley boy ascends the mainmast and saves the mickey. Norman's tenacity to pursue an object acts as a foil to Hilliot who wavers and fails to crystallise impulses into an action. He resembles T.S. Eliot's Prufrock who says:

"Do I dare
Disturb the universe?"[1]

He wants to beat up Andy for his acrimonious relationship with him but he shrinks from doing what he feels. He says, "...I fear to greatly decisive action in an emotional crisis of calibre; nor do I wish to admit myself that I consider Andy sufficiently important; but this, as you say, is clearly enough a case of self-defence—."[2] Hilliot suffers from frustration and ignominy at his discomfiture. Thus Hilliot becomes a butt of ridicule in the eyes of shipmates on account of his awful isolation from the shipping community.

The affront he receives at the hands of Andy and other shipmates fills him with anguish from the very beginning of his voyage. The anguish becomes acute all the more when in course of his voyage, before he reaches Tsjang-Tsjang, he either remains on the deck of the ship lost in the world of drink, or if he goes ashore, he boozes there too. All other shipmates run after girls in brothels and drink to their fill to beguile the tedium of journey by sea. He considers it to be a sacrilege to run after girls because of the pledge of fidelity to Janet.

This commitment to Janet is also one of the prime reasons of his estrangement from shipmates. The sense of alienation mounts in him and his link with Janet too snaps, when he does not receive a letter from Janet for weeks together. In his soliloquy, he says, "But let us have no nonsense about it. The

1. Eliot, T.S : *Selected Poems*, p. 12.
2. Lowry, Malcolm: *Ultramarine*, p. 134.

memory of your virginity fills me with disgust. Disgust and contempt!...Good God, I loathe you, abwhore you, Janet."[1]

This relationship between Hilliot and Janet is reminiscent of relationship between Benjamin Hall and Eva in Nordahl Grieg's *The Ship Sails On.* The influence of *The Ship Sails On,* published in 1927, is so profound on the mind of Malcolm Lowry that his Dana Hilliot has his germ in Benjamin Hall and Janet her germ in Eva. As Benjamin Hall misses his sweetheart on the deck of Mignon, Dana Hilliot pines for his love Janet on the deck of the Oedipus Tyrannus. Grieg's protagonist prays that there will be a letter from his sweetheart waiting for him in Cape Town. When there is no letter, he angrily goes ashore with the crew, bent on erasing his memory of Eva by boozing and indulging himself in sexual orgy. As a delayed letter reaches both Dana Hilliot and his counterpart Benjamin Hall, they find themselves launched on a course of life that has set them adrift from all their moorings. It is said of Benjamin. "Now everything was finished... the tears slowly trickled down his cheeks. He was so hopelessly young and unhappy, so faint and shattered by life's cruel blow. He was only nineteen, a little clod of soft spring-time mould after all."[2]

Dana Hilliot too steps ashore and with Hans Popplereuter, a German wireless operator, stranded at Tsjang-Tsjang, goes to pubs and brothels and dances with Olga Sologub, a Russian refugee prostitute, in disregard of his promise to Janet that he will not be ensnared by any woman. Dana Hillot, roaming the centres of fleshpots in the port town of Tsjang-Tsjang, is also atrocious in view of his not heeding the stern precept at the Anatomical Museum 'The Wages of Sin is Death'. The novelist's portrait of Dana Hilliot is that of a man who suffers alienation in Satre's existential epistemology and is striving hard to discover some sort of harmony with life.

This search for an identity is through the everlasting fire of hell. He is so fallen into the quagmire of vile passions that he thinks of carrying the Russian prostitute to the ship and

1. *Ibid.*, p. 51.
2. Quoted in Douglas Day's *Malcolm Lowry: A Biography*, p. 118.

hiding her in his bunk. Perhaps the suggestion that emanated from his grandfather's eyes in picture to him "Don't listen to what she says, son. The sea will get you as it got me"[1] has come true. The sea has overwhelmed Dana Hilliot. He loses Janet't letter and this casual treatment shows up the hollowness of his love for Janet.

It appears that Hilliot has been spinning a lofty conception of love but when it boils down to the facts of life, he fumbles and falters. Daniel B Dodson rightly says of Hilliot's relationship with Janet: "their relationship has consisted of nothing more bestial than clutched hands and the brush of chaste lips. Fearing sex and contamination, Dana Hilliot turns to alcohol and onanism..."[2] His fear of a full-blooded sexual relationship prevents him from accepting Olga Sologub's invitation to come upstairs for the gratification of sensual appetite.

It is not the remembrance of Janet's letter that sends a deep wave of nostalgia, but physical sickness resulting from his dread of having a full-blooded relationship that sweeps over him and makes him stagger and fall. A man, who round and round swings rhythmically with Olga Sologub, says to her in a mood of nonchalance: "But give me half an hour. I want to cool my brain a little and think."[3]

Dana Hilliot is a typical modern man for whom love degenerates into lust recalling a love scene in T.S. Eliot's *The Fire Sermon* section of *The Waste Land.* Even the gratification of sensual appetite is inhibited by Hilliot's sexual perversity of onanism and this incapacity to have sexual virility reminds the reader of T.S. Eliot's *Gerontion:*

> "These with a thousand small deliberations
> Protract the profit of their chilled delirium,
> Excite the membrane, when the sense has cooled,
> With pungent sauces, multiply variety
> In a wilderness of mirrors."[4]

1. Lowry, Malcolm: *Ultramarine*, p. 119.
2. Dodson, B Daniel: *Malcolm Lowry* (Columbia University Press), p. 8.
3. Lowry, Malcolm: *Ultramarine*, p. 116.
4. Eliot, T.S.: *Selected Poems*, p. 33.

Dana Hilliot's encounter with Olga Sologub shows that the flame of passion does not burn in him in all its incandescence and it will not be an exaggeration, if we discover an affinity between Dana Hilliot and Gerontion (the difference in the age of the two is glaring, the former a youngman of nineteen and the latter an oldman) who says "I have lost my passion."[1]

Dana Hilliot does not make any confession that his passions are spent but when we come to his relationship with women like his sweetheart Janet and the Russian prostitute Olga Sologub, his amorous relationship is anaemic and is emblematic of the desiccation of personality wrought by the thirties. The parallel between Malcolm Lowry's Dana Hilliot and Eliot's spiritually sick Gerontion is also in keeping with Eliot's influence on the mind of Malcolm Lowry.

Dana Hilliot like Grieg's Benjamin Hall is obsessed with the mortal disease of syphilis. In one of his interior disclosures he speaks with remarkable candour of his preoccupation with disease: "Dana Hilliot, the syphilitic, as he strolls aimfully down Great Homer Street. Look! How everyone he touches is smitten with the dire disease.[2] His mind is so much defiled with filth, squalor and stench that he constructs ugly fantasies about his relatives and parents: "All his father, brothers and sisters had died, obscurely, but venerably, in early infancy; and his father is now in a home eating the buttons off the chair at Clairaudient intervals, and composing a Sonnet Sequence, Songs of Second Childhood..."[3], while his mother is going blind.

In this state of mind when the fear of the dire disease and the estrangement from Janet rankles in his mind, he suffers indignity again at the hands of the Cook Andy who crowns him a frying pan, when he tells him that the pie is lousy. He sees no way out of this traumatic experience but to make away with Andy. First he gives vent to his pent-up fury by hurling a reproach at Andy but a change comes over Hilliot. He feels remorse for Andy.

1. *Ibid.*, p. 33.
2. Lowry, Malcolm: *Ultramarine*, p. 73.
3. *Ibid.*, p. 72.

Out of this remorse comes strange, wistful tenderness for everybody, for the ship and even for his home. This is perhaps a crucial experience in his life. It is a watershed dividing the Hilliot of dismal prospects obsessed with the feeling that he is the human husk, the leaf of ash, from the Hilliot who has 'a perfectly clear vision of himself'[1]—Plodding towards "the summer, towards those burning seas of light."[2]

The awareness of making up his quarrel with Andy leading to his acceptance by the community of the ship is a prelude to the epiphany in the final chapter of the novel when he elects "To sail into an unknown spring, or receive his baptism on storm's promontory."[3] This epiphany or spot of time is born out of Hilliot's relationship with a minor character Andy in the novel. W.J. Harvey says, "The problem of bridging the gap, of modulating without obvious strain or incongruity from the intense to the relaxed, the exceptional to the mundane might seem to be primarily one of style."[4]

Malcolm Lowry succeeds in correlating the intensity of the epiphany with the ordinary, day-to-day, concerns of the moral life in terms of the character relationship of Dana Hilliot and Andy. Hilliot has shed all illusions and his clear-eyed vision informs his character with humility. He is now no longer treated a toff and he too in his turn has a rapport with them. He wants to save Norman's mickey from death in the shark-infested harbour but Andy prevents him from putting his life in peril. This is not a forced resolution of acrimonious relationship between Hilliot and Andy. In his letter to Janet he says "I have identification with Andy: I am Andy. I regard it all now with sanity and detachment."[5] He further tells Janet that he has also outgrown Andy owing to his being in love with her.

Their private love has developed into a universal experience of sublimated all-embracing love for mankind. Though

1. *Ibid.*, p. 185.
2. *Ibid.*, p. 201.
3. *Ibid.*, p. 201.
4. Harvey, W.J.: *Character and the Novel*, (Cornell University Press, 1969), p. 65.
5. Lowry, Malcolm: *Ultramarine*, p. 185.

Malcolm Lowry finds the germ of Dana Hilliot in some measure in Nordahl Grieg's Benjamin Hall, his portrayal of Dana Hilliot is richer than that of Nordahl Grieg's. Grieg's *The Ship Sails On* is ridden with disease and guilt. Benjamin Hall is haunted by an all-consuming guilt that he has killed Anton and the counterpart of Dana Hilliot in Grieg's novel is self-destructive. The ship is a filthy, floating shell concealing in its bowels a real inferno. The Oedipus Tyrannus too is 'a sort of Moloch.'[1] And Hilliot himself confesses that, "Each port had roared its smutty laugh at him, bringing him nearer and nearer to his own little destruction."[2]

But he also owes a debt to the Oedipus Tyrannus, because when he became a part of the shipping community, all loose tangles of his life were set straight and he says it was the 'strong, generous ship he knew, he must thank for giving it to him."[3] It was on the ship that the maelstrom of noise, of tangled motion was succeeded by a clear perception of the pitiless regularity of the moving bars. And he saw that at last the interdependence of rod, grasping rod, had become related to his meaning and his own struggles. At the end he becomes a fireman on the Oedipus Tyrannus, because he feels that the firemen seemed in some queer way to be nearer to God. Douglas Day rightly says that "There is no salvation, or exaltation, by solitary ascent to heaven. There is only humanity, and the fellowship of the inferno as one's reward for manifesting his humanity somewhere, below, God exists."[4]

The inverted apocalyptic vision Dana Hilliot sees has some affinity with that of a Graham Greene novel in which characters through inferno move towards beatitude. Like Greene's Scobie in *The Heart of the Matter* Dana Hilliot chose evil with eyes open. Malcolm Lowry's portrait of Dana Hilliot is informed with Conrad Aiken's ethic developed by Demarest in *Blue Voyage*: "Why do we all want to be

1. *Ibid.*, p. 41.
2. *Ibid.*, p. 157.
3. *Ibid.*, p. 170.
4. *Ibid.*. p. 23.

crucified, to fling ourselves into the very heart of the flame? Empedocles on Etna. A moment of incandescent suffering. To suffer intensely is to live intensely, to be intensely conscious... passionate, perverse refusal to give up the unattainable—dashing ourselves blindly against the immortal wall, "I will be crucified! Here are my hands! Drive nails through them—sharp blows!"[1]

(C) TECHNIQUE

Ultramarine was published in 1933 and the thirties in the sphere of fiction witnessed an abatement of rigorous concern for form discernible in the works of Henry James, Conrad and James Joyce. With the relaxing of immense artistic preoccupations of novelists of the nineties and the first two decades of the twentieth century is observable a reversion to the native tradition of English novel of Defoe and Fielding. Malcolm Bradbury rightly comments: "We often presume, in modern criticism, that in the English line the experimental tradition did shift or lapse, a lapse usually identified with the thirties, when realism and politics came back, and a generation less certain of its artistic role—writers with the Silver Age presumptions of Waugh's Gilbert Pinfold or the uneasy anti-aestheticism of an Orwell, the guilt of a Virginia Woolf, the self-diminution of an Isherwood, sacrificially offering sensitivity to an overwhelming historical experience—gives us a 'contemporary' rather than a 'modern' fiction."[2] The desire for experimentation in the field of fiction has given way to a desire for informing novel with the social and cultural milieu of the civilization.

It is a shift in emphasis but Lowry's *Ultramarine* is perhaps an exception to the shift in emphasis that has come over English fiction. It is because the power that shapes his craft of fiction resides not in England but across the Altantic in Conrad Aiken, an American novelist of the thirties. When the

1. Aiken, Conrad: *Blue Voyage*, (McGraw Hill Book Company, New York), pp. 23-4.
2. *Possibilities*, p. 86.

wave of innovation and experimentation subsides in England, it creates a ferment in the mind of American novelists. Thus a discussion of technique in *Ultramarine* has to be correlated with the unremitting search for form in American fiction in the thirties, especially in Conrad Aiken's *Blue Voyage* that becomes a mental wardrobe of Lowry. In Author's Preface to *Three Novels* Conrad Aiken says about himself, "Form was certainly to be a prime desideratum, yes."[1] Form too becomes a preoccupation with Lowry, when excepting novelists like Samuel Beckett and Lawrence Durrell, all other English novelists of the thirties have gone in for traditional realism.

The preoccupation with form is perhaps in the sense of 'technique' as defined by Mark Schcrer in the essay *Technique as Discovery*. Technique in fiction, according to Mark Schorer, is not a supplementary element that adds embellishment to the content. In blunter terms it is not the arrangement of events to create a plot, suspense, climax and the analysis of character motivation. Technique is not something external to the content but it is the only means at the disposal of a novelist "...Of discovering, exploring, developing his subject, of conveying its meaning, and, finally, of evaluating it."[2] It becomes a tool towards the positive definition of the theme.

Its importance is all the more imperative for the writer of *Ultramarine* who is intensely involved in the experience which forms the stuff of the novel. The material out of which the novel is built is purely personal. It is a fictional analogue for his experiences as a deckboy on the Pyrrhus bcund for Far East, when he leaves the school, the Leys, at the age of seventeen. His nautical experiences as a deckboy for six months become the experiences of Dana Hilliot on the Oedipus Tyrannus in *Ultramarine*.

The novel is thus autobiographical and an autobiographical novel runs the risk of becoming a riot of emotions and shapeless, unless there is an in-built mechanism that assimilates experiences and forms a coherent whole. The

1. Aiken, C ırad: *Three Novels*, p 4.
2. *Perspectives on Fiction*, Edited by James L. Calderwood and Harold E Tolivei (Oxford University Press, 1968), p. 200.

in-built mechanism is technique that after a scrutiny of the powerful emotions, suffering and passion of the writer imposes an order on them. Lowry discovers this importance of technique in making an introspection of his feelings and organising them into a pattern in Conrad Aiken's *Blue Voyage*. To Conrad Aiken the novel becomes a tool of coming to grips with problems plaguing him: "Here was the artist-hero-servant in a new predicament: he could understand his neurosis, and then proceed to create with it, on the one hand, while he analysed both the neurosis and himself away with the other."[1] Lowry's technique in *Ultramarine* is a tool analysing and giving a shape to neuroses gnawing at his heart.

This mode of talking about the sickness of one's own heart is reminiscent of D.H. Lawrence, especially in his autobiographical novel *Sons and Lovers*. Lawrence talls us about his deep emotional involvement in his fictional representatives: "One sheds one's sickness in books, repeats and presents again one's emotions to be master of them."[2] As Paul becomes the fictional analogue of D.H. Lawrence in *Sons and Lovers*, Dana Hilliot, journeying by the Oedipus Tyrannus, becomes the representative of Lowry journeying by the Pyrrhus. In both the novelists we find a tale of their personal predicament; in the former the crippling effect of the mother on his mind and in the latter the painful fact of alienation not only from parents but from the crew of the Oedipus Tyrannus and life in general. It is not a mere record of the neuroses that afflict them but also an attempt at mastering them. The technique here has got a therapeutic value not for the reader but for the writer himself curing him of his sickness.

The technique, Lowry employs for portraying and mastering his personal predicament, works in terms of the stream-of-consciousness and flash-back. "The technique of the stream-of-consciousness is a subtle way of recapturing memories, thoughts and feelings that in the words of William James exist "outside the primary consciousness."[3] This technique puts an

1. Aiken, Conrad: *Three Novels*, p. 5.
2. Quoted by Mark Schorer *in Perspectives on Fiction*, p. 207.
3. Quoted by Robert Humphrey in *Perspectives on Fiction*, p. 253.

emphasis on exploration of the inchoate "prespeech level of consciousness for the purpose, primarily, of revealing the psychic being of the characters."[1] It is plumbing the depth of the psyche beneath the surface of the conscious mind. It is also because in the words of Virginia Woolf "Life is...a luminous halo, a semi-transparent envelope surrounding us from the beginning of consciousness to the end."[2] And the business of the novelist using the technique of consciousness is to convey this varying, this unknown and uncircumscribed spirit.

Instead of commenting in his own person, Lowry makes the reader browse through the chamber of consciousness of his protagonist Dana Hilliot in *Ultramarine.* This technique of the stream-of-consciousness enables the novelist to present Dana Hilliot who is in a constant state of unstable equilibrium and whose mood is never anything static but a fluid pattern mixing memory with desire. In Chapter One at one place Dana Hilliot is gazing at the fireman when three bells ring. He becomes forgetful of his presence in the midst of the crew and becomes melancholy and descends into the labyrinth of his psyche: "What sorrow was it, stirring in his mind behind the screen of time? A note of memory merely growing fainter, drowning in the yellow sea of his consciousness? Ah, but no, he had it, and following it, he suddenly saw a small boy, himself three years ago, inkstains on his fingers, sitting upon the steps of the swimming baths at school, his eyes burning.... Forlorn: The very word is like a bell. To toll me back from thee to my sad self. What could it have been that reminded him? The engine, possibly, of the steam heater, that pounded there all day to warm the baths. Green Water. It had been like plunging into moss....Left out of the swimming team, the important match against Uppingham. He had stolen out of last period to have a look on the notice board. A smell of peat smoke from the fens. He had got up when he saw

1. *Perspectives on Fiction* Edited by James L. Calderwood and Harold E. Toliver (Oxford University Press, 1968), p. 255.
2. Quoted by Robert Humphrey in *Perspectives on Fiction*, p. 262.

two prefects coming down past the Hall, early from the Doctor's Greek Testament Class:...how did it go?"[1]

This interior monologue of Hilliot is a recurrent motif from the beginning to the end of the novel. In the soliloquy we find Dana Hilliot in his real self, when he becomes oblivious of the outside world and like Keats in 'Ode to a Nightingale' is seized with his sole self. 'Forlorn' is the word he adapts from Keats' Ode for illuminating his solitary state of mind. In the monologue he analyzes himself and sees visions. The stream-of-consciousness technique enables the novelist to peel off the veil of external reality concealing the care of the personality of the protagonist Dana Hilliot and to give the visionary gleam he seizes. To Lowry as well as to Conrad Aiken vision is the primary thing. Lowry perhaps is in full rapport with Conrad Aiken who says that without vision "no amount of observation, or cataloguing, or mere naming, or immersion in the thingness of the thing—that insidiously destructive bequest of William Carlos Williams—can ever add up to any sort of totality of response to the universe with which we are faced, outer and inner."[2]

This totality of response to the outer and inner reality is possible through the use of the technique of stream-of-consciousness. The external reality of the carpenter on the deck of the Oedipus Tyrannus in *Ultramarine* engenders a rich association of image in Dana Hilliot. The carpenter on the deck takes Dana Hilliot to the carpenter, the father of Christ, to Christ himself and Christ playing with nails in Nazareth makes him imagine the crucifixion of Christ bringing redemption to the sinning humanity. And Dana Hilliot seeks deliverance: "Oh Lord God, look down on your unworthy and unwashed servant, Hilliot, the seaman, the Liverpool—Norwegian, whose knees knock together at thunder, whose filthy hands tremble always in impotent prayer; . . . and as he stands alone, naked, weaponless, deliver him from his bondage and bring him out of the darkness and the grief and

1. Lowry, Malcolm: *Ultramarine*, p. 24.
2. Aiken, Conrad: Author's Preface, *Three Novels*, p. 5.

pain into sunlight."[1] The important constituents of the stream-of-consciousness include intuition, vision and sometimes the occult. And Dana Hilliot the protagonist in *Ultramarine* is very much prone to see visions.

Lowry also makes use of the technique of expressionism, a variant of the stream-of-consciousness. Expressionism is non-mimetic and therefore in revolt against Realism, Naturalism and Impressionism. In Herbert Read's words the Expressionist artist does not wish to reproduce "the objective reality of the world, but the subjective reality of the feelings which objects and events arouse...."[2] For the Expressionist the truth resides not in the observable world but in the mind of the perceiver and on account of Lowry's this conception of the universe he has to take recourse to the expressionist technique that works in terms of 'fantasy-thinking'.[3] Fantasy-thinking, as Jung feels, is different from "a thinking that is adapted to reality, by means of which we imitate the successiveness of objectively real things..."[4]

Malcolm Lowry's technique in *Ultramarine* is not an imitation of the successiveness of objectively real things. But it does not mean that he is a romancer weaving only fanciful tales. Gerald Noxon, one of Lowry's closest literary friends at Cambridge, rightly says that Lowry discards the 'aridity of a purely realistic style'[5] and goes in for dream-thinking. His protagonist in *Ultramarine* speaks through images and dreams.

It is this language of dream and myth that makes him come to grips with the painful fact of his alienation. It is perhaps that "in the deeper layers of the unconscious there is a formative principle at work, moulding some primordial material of the psyche into icons."[6] It is this technique of fashioning an icon out of materia primordialis of the

1. Lowry, Malcolm: *Ultramarine*, p. 77.
2. Read, Herbert: *The Philosophy of Modern Art*, p. 51.
3. Read, Herbert: *Art Now*, p. 102.
4. Quoted by Herbert Read in *Art Now*, p. 103.
5. Day, Douglas: *Malcolm Lowry: A Biography*, p. 102.
6. Read, Herbert; *Art Now*, p. 105.

unconscious that Lowry presents Dana Hilliot ascending from the inferno of despair into the forecastle of the Oedipus Tyrannus: "Lost in an unfamiliar dream, when spirit becomes filled with stars, instead of wounds, and good and compassionate and tender."[1]

This stands in a sharp contrast with the first-person narrative of Dana Hilliot in Chapter III telling us about all pervasive snow benumbing life: "North wind blow south over my vineyards, north wind brings the snow, I do not think that there is the north wind. Snow, on the high pitched minster roof and spire; snow on the boughs of leafless linden trees; snow on the silent streets and squares that freeze...Drowsed are the voices of droned litanies. Blurred as in dreams the voice of priest and friar. Cold hath numbed sense to slumber here....Snow fell softly across my dream..."[2]

Lowry's technique of stream-of-consiousness owes much to his tutor Conrad Aiken but, "he had a powerful mind—more powerful, perhaps even than Aiken's—and one of the delights of his fiction could be the spectacle of that mind examining itself."[3] The sharp critical intelligence of Lowry makes him avoid the two extremes of the realistic style of Zola and personal stenography of James Joyce and develops a style that moves up and down the corridors of the psyche of his character and viewing his journey with a reasonable measure of detachment. When Lowry has Dana Hilliot, in a passage reflect that "what one writes, if one is to be any good, must be rooted in some sort of autochthony,"[4] and then admit that he is incapable of creating anything intended to have its own life outside himself, he was performing a very shrewd self-diagonsis —both as man and as novelist. The shrewd self-diagnosis saves his interior disclosures from being an indulgence in subjectivity noticeable in Chapter IV of Conrad Aiken's *Blue Voyage* in which Demarest, the artist protagonist, is weaving the tale of

1. Lowry, Malcolm: *Ultramarine*, p. 201.
2. *Ibid.*, pp. 125-6.
3. Day, Douglas: *Malcolm Lowry: A Biography*, pp. 171-2.
4. Lowry, Malcolm: *Ultramarine*, p, 96.

a monotonous journey through his forlorn self of the deck of the ship.

A typically important feature of Lowry's technique in *Ultramarine* is his imbedding the text with phrases from the works of authors such as Shakespeare, Keats and T.S. Eliot. We find this technique in T.S. Eliot's poetry used for the sake of setting up an ironic contrast between two different modes of life. In Malcolm Lowry it is used for a different purpose. It evokes an intense association of feeling and thought. Keats' lines "Forlorn'! the very word is like a bell/ To toll me back from thee to my sole self,"[1] figure in Chapter One in *Ultramarine* with the word 'Sole' replaced by 'Sad'. Shakespeare's line "Never, never, never, never, never,"[2] in *King Lear* occurs in Chapter Two of *Ultramarine.* This Shakespearean tag occurs to Dana Hilliot's mind, when he finds that his pledge of fidelity to Janet is under strain and his old relation of purity is going to be snapped for good. T.S. Eliot's lines:

> "I should have been a pair of ragged claws
> Scuttling across the floors of silent seas."[3]

in *The Love Song of J.Alfred Prufrock* are adapted by Malcolm Lowry in *Ultramarine* with a variation: "I wish I were. I wish I were—what? A pair of ragged clauses scuttling between two dark parentheses?"[4] Both Dana Hilliot and Prufrock have a craving for a noble mission. Dana Hilliot wants to whip the sea and Prufrock desires to disturb the universe but something ails them. Instances of this nature can be catalogued but my objective is not to ferret out all such expressions of other authors used by Lowry in *Ultramarine.* The three instances already cited tell us about the typical modern technique of Malcolm Lowry.

1. Keats, John: Ode to a Nightingale, *The Golden Treasury* Edited by John Press, p. 248.
2. Shakespeare, William: *King Lear*, Globe Edition, p. 933.
3 *Selected Poems*, p. 14.
4. Lowry, Malcolm: *Ultramarine*, p. 143.

Ultramarine has a musical organization. This musical organization Malcolm Lowry assimilates from Conrad Aiken's counter-pointing of syncopated dialogue and interior monologue. The Smoking-room scenes in Conrad Aiken's *Blue Voyage* with their juxtaposed conversations, that bear on one another only in an oblique manner, find their echo in the fo'c'sle scenes of Lowry's *Ultramarine*. Lowry's experiments with syncopated dialogue in his first novel *Ultramarine* anticipate his deft use of the technique in such crucial scenes of *Under the Volcano* relating to Yvonne's return at the outset of Chapter Two and the final episode in the Farolito.

From the very first novel the impression gains ground that Malcolm Lowry feels more at home in the exploration of mental processes than in the depiction of external reality. It is to the credit of Malcoln Lowry that his use of interior monologue, instead of being a purple patch, becomes integrated with the complex forces at work in the psyche of his protagonist Dana Hilliot.

The interweaving of the motifs of guilt, longing and fear of death is reminiscent of Stephen's night-town experience and its fall-out in James Joyce's novel *A Portrait of the Artist*. That porcrayal of the tangled web of mental processes, the forte of Malcolm Lowry is evident in impressions swarming Dana Hilliot's consciousness, when he imagines himslf with Janet at the end of Chapter One in *Ultramarine*: "Then he was walking again with Janet slowly through the crowd. Electric lights swam fast. Gas jets crocus-coloured, steadily flared and whirred. The shouts and cries of the market rose and fell about them like the breathing of a monster. Above, the moon soared and galloped through a dark tempestuous sky. All at once, every lamp in the street exploded, their globes flew out, darted into the sky, and the street became alive with eyes; eyes greatly dilated, dripping dry scurf, or glued with viscid gum; eyes which held eternity in the fixedness of their stare; eyes which wavered, and spread, and, diminishing rapidly, were catapulted east and west; eyes that were the gutted windows of a cathedral, blackened emptiness of the brain, through which bats and ravens wheeled enormously, leathern foulnesses, heeling over in the dry winds; but one eye plunged up at him from the morass, stared at him unwinkingly. It was the eye of a pigeon, moist and alone, crying."[1]

1. Lowry, Malcolm: *Ultramarine*, p. 44.

3

Under the Volcano

Son of man,
You cannot say, or guess, for you know only
A heap of broken images, where the Sun beats,
And the dead tree gives no shelter, the cricket no relief,
And the dry stone no sound of water.

—T.S. Eliot: *The Waste Land*

(A) DOMINANT THEMES

Lowry's second novel *Under the Volcano* (1947) centres round Geoffrey Firmin, the British Consul, in the Mexican town Quauhnahuac between twin Volcanoes Popocatepetl and Ixtaccihuatl. Like Joyce's *Ulysses,* Lowry's *Under the Volcano* deals with the events of a single day in the life of its protagonist Geoffrey Firmin. The British Consul finds that on the Mexican Day of the Dead, November 1938, his wife Yvonne, who has divorced him, comes from America to renew their marriage. Yvonne had left Geoffrey Firmin on account of his insatiable lust for wine but after eighteen months one fine morning she comes to the husband to make reparations for the rupture of their marital relations. Geoffrey Firmin rejects her love and fails to ! ave conjugal felicity with Yvonne. He forsakes Yvonne's love for the sake of the pleasures of wine.

When this story of Geoffrey Firmin and Yvonne comes out, many reviewers take it for the tale of a dipsomaniac who spurns the offer of love held out by his wife. It is a fact that *Under the Volcano* is a book in which for three quarters of the time the hero is drunk and moves in the realm of a phantasmagoria. If the protagonist feels tight for three quarters of the time, some may legitimately protest that the novel is not about normal life and it appears to be a case history of an individual. But a sensitive engagement with the text reveals just the reverse of the feelings of casual readers looking upon *Under the Volcano* as the tale of neurosis plaguing the British Consul in the Mexican town. A reader who is responsive to 'the multi-valued poetic fiction'[1] of *Under the Volcano* feels that, though the overt external action is slight from seven in the morning to seven in the evening, "it takes on a heavy symbolic weight which must be felt in its relation to the symbolism of numerous objects, properties, occurrences and even ideas, and recollections and observations."[2] Instead of becoming the case history of a drunk, it becomes the story of a civilization in which all are drunk: "Good God, if our civilization were to sober up for a couple of days it'd die of remorse on the third."[3] The tale of an individual assumes a universal character pointing to people seized with a frenzy reeling toward destruction.

This frenzy is the result of the primacy of the ego in man and Geoffrey makes a correct diagnosis of the malady that afflicts him and goads him inexorably to turn his back on his wife Yvonne who has come to repair his shattered self. It is the 'tyranny of self'[4] that is eating into his vitals and he wants a deliverance and unless he seeks deliverance from utter subjection to his solitary self, he remains in hell. This captivity of the human mind into the dingy cell of pure subjectivity is one of the primary themes of the novel. The predicament of

1. The Sewanee Review, Vol. LV (1974), p. 492.
2. *Ibid.*, p. 488.
3. Lowry, Malcolm: *Under the Volcano*, p. 117.
4. *Ibid.*, p. 289.

an individual enslaved by his ego finds an expression in the poetry of the thirties. T.S. Eliot in *The Waste Land* says:

> "I have heard the key
> Turn in the door once and turn once only
> We think of the key, each in his prison
> Thinking of the key, each confirms a prison"[1]

When an individual finds himself trapped in the shackles of his self, cut off from the rest of the community of men, he finds himself in a veritable hell. Geoffrey's unsent letter to Yvonne in Chapter One of the novel tells us how intensely Geoffrey yearns for Yvonne: "If I am to survive I need your help[2] but he falters and fumbles when the question of seeking succour from her arises by posting the letter. He very sensitively recreates how he is stuck up in the labyrinth of his individual self: "And why did I not send a telegram or some word immediately? Ah, why not, why not, why not? For I suppose you would have come back in due course if I had asked you. But this is what it is to live in hell. I could not, cannot ask you. I could not, cannot send a telegram."[3] This imprisonment of the individual in the dungeon of his own making results from the desiccation of values that weave people into an organic community.

The absence of an organic community is acutely felt in the writers of the nineties and the first two decades of the twentieth century. Every writer is in search of a myth or symbol that gives coherence and meaning to his work. James Joyce, D.H. Lawrence, W.B. Yeats and T.S. Eliot in their own ways are engaged in a quest for a system of their own, because no universally acceptable system is there. Stephen Spender's comment is quite apt: "...*Under the Volcano* has to be considered in the context of the Europe of the nineteen twenties and nineteen thirties which produced *Ulysses*, *The*

1. *Selected Poems*, p. 67.
2. Lowry, Malcolm: *Under the Volcano*, p. 38.
3. *Ibid.*, p. 38.

Wasteland, *The Orators*, and other books about the breakdown of values."[1]

On account of this breakdown of values the writings of this period deal with characters who are locked up inside the caves of their minds. They feel suffocated and sometimes are impelled by an urge to discover some abiding values. When Dana Hilliot in *Ultramarine* feels puzzled at the sight of a world lacking in order and coherence he feels the necessity of clutching at something that will save him from appalling isolation. Geoffrey in *Under the Volcano* is engaged in writing a book *Secret Knowledge* and the question of absolutes in life becomes his central concern: "Is there any ultimate reality, external, conscious and ever-present etc. etc. that can be realised by any such means that may be acceptable to all creeds and religions and suitable to all climes and countries?"[2]

His search for the eternal verities of life fails, because his obsession with his private self is irresistible and of this preoccupation he speaks to Yvonne in his unsent epistle: "Or do you find me between Mercy and Understanding, between Chesed and Binah (but still at Chesed)—my equilibrium, and equilibrium is all, precarious—balancing, teetering over the awful unbridgeable void, the all—but unretraceable path of God's lightning back to God? As if I ever were in Chesed! More like the Oliphoth."[3]

The reference in this passage to Binah, Chesed and Oliphoth brings in the mystery of the Cabbala. The Cabbala adds a new dimension to the theme of the 'tyranny of self' that has made a wreck of the life of Geoffrey. It adds a resonance to the theme of Geoffrey Firmin's descent into inferno. According to Zohar, the sacred book of the Cabbala, God makes His divinity felt to the mortals by ten emanations. The ten emanations of God in the Cabbala are like Plato's Intelligences acting as a bridge between the celestial order and the temporal world. The spark that emanates from God "is arranged hierarchically from spiritual down to physical states

1. Spender, Stephen: *Introduction* to *Under the Volcano*, p. viii.
2. Lowry, Malcolm: *Under the Volcano*, p. 39.
3. *Ibid.*, p. 39.

in an intricate structure and is known as the Sephirotic Tree...".[1] The Tree is composed of Kether, the Crown; Chochma, Wisdom; and Binah, Understanding.

A man has a perception of this triad, if he is chaste and abstemious but as soon as he violates the Law, he can go no higher than the second triad: "Chesed, Mercy; Geburah, Power; and Tipheret, Wordly Glory."[2] Generally, people become enamoured of the lower branches of the tree in the material world of appetite and passion. When sensual appetites get the better of man, the Tree is turned upside down and the sinner's climb towards heaven becomes a slide into Oliphoth, the realm of husks and demons. And Geoffrey's slide into the underworld of husks and demons is emblematic of those who violate the Law.

In Chapter Two Yvonne's expectations are that she will embark on a new life with Geoffrey but she suffers disillusionment and in the tone of a supplicant wants to know from Geoffrey: "Must you go on and on for ever into this stupid darkness, seeking it, even now, where I cannot reach you, ever on into the darkness of the sundering of the Severance!—Oh Geoffrey, why do you do it!"[3] But Geoffrey feels measureless exhilaration when he is drunk. Instead of agreeing with Yvonne that a cantina is a cave of darkness, he considers it to be the fount of celestial joy: "Forgive me, no. Not so much the beauty of this one necessarily, which a regression on my part, is not perhaps properly a cantina but think of all the terrible ones where people go mad that will soon be taking down their shutters, for not even the gates of heaven, opening wide to receive me, could fill me with such celestial complicated and hopeless joy as the iron screen that rolls up with a crash; as the unpadlocked jostling jalousies which admit those whose souls tremble with the drink they carry unsteadily to their lips. All mystery, all hope, all disappointment, yes, all disaster is here beyond those swinging doors."[4]

1. Day, Douglas: *Malcolm Lowry: A Biography*, p. 344.
2. *Ibid.*, p. 344.
3. Lowry, Malcolm: *Under the Volcano*, p. 50.
4. *Ibid.*, p. 50.

From this account of Geoffrey Firmin it appears that drink that gives him a thrill, also makes him slide down hill into the pit of disaster. This account of a drunk treading the path of ruin gives the lie to critics who hold that Geoffrey is a mere alcoholic wreck. Conrad KnickerBocker cites a line from Lowry explaining his fondness for wine: "The real cause of alcoholism is the complete baffling sterility of existence as sold to you."[1] He has something Faustian about him and he becomes an exemplar of the theme of destruction brought about by egoism and self-love. This theme of egoism and self-regarding love is not peculiar to an age but common to humanity irrespective of time and space.

Douglas Day's analysis of the theme of auto-destruction revealed through the character of Geoffrey is quite incisive.... "It is a frenzied and headlong leap into the abyss, a deliberate and successful attempt at self-damnation. This failed Consul, this erratic and faintly ludicrous drunk, is nothing less than a modern-day type of the Faustian—Promethean rebel, a man who turns his back on Grace, and who seeks by doing so to acquire diabolical wisdom and power. He knows, like Rimbaud, Baudelaire, and the rest of the poetes maudits, that the way down and the way up are one and the same; and he, like them, prefers the way down."[2] This theme of self-damnation is stated in the First Chapter of the novel that acts as a prologue to the book. M. Laruelle, a former French Film-Director and a boyhood friend of Geoffrey, in course of his sojourn with Geoffrey in the town of Quauhnahuac, tells us about Marlowe's Faustus who like Geoffrey Firmin treads the path of perdition by striking a bargain with infernal powers for the sake of the sweet sensations of body.

As Marlowe's Faustus could not pray for Grace, Geoffrey cannot feel a love that might break his love for alcohol, or rather symbolising a saving-attitude. Thus Geoffrey is akin to Marlowe's Faustus who sins against the Holy Ghost by mingling pride with despair.

1. Quoted by Stephen Spender in Introduction to *Under the Volcano*, p. xxiii.
2. Day, Douglas: *Malcolm Lowry: A Biography*, p. 345.

The theme of despair presented through the character of Geoffrey is theological. It is begotten in man when he severes his relationship with the source of his religion. This estrangement from religion results in a man's refusal to love or be loved. This impulse of refusal to love is fed by his pride. This theme finds a support in the inscription on the wall of the house of M. Laruelle. The inscription, "No se puede vivir sin amar," (We cannot live without loving), brings home to the reader that Geoffrey who feels like a "ravaged and stricken town"[1], because he is incapable of loving anything other than his own tyrannical self.

The pathos of his agonised self when Yvonne is away from him is deeply moving in a scene in the company of his friend Dr. Vigil in a church in Quauhnahuac: "...he did't know, with sombre tapestries, and strange votive pictures, a compassionate Virgin floating in the gloom, to whom he prayed, with muddily beating heart, he might have Yvonne again. Dark figures, tragic and isolated, stood about the Church, or were kneeling —only the bereaved and lonely went there." "She is the Virgin for those who have nobody with", the doctor told him inclining his head toward the image. "And for mariners on the sea."[2]

Geoffrey is one of the bereaved and the lonely and prays in silence before the Virgin. This is when Yvonne is away, and when she comes back, he rejects her. He is now praying before another Virgin: "Nothing is altered and in spite of God's mercy I am still alone. Though my suffering seems senseless I am still in agony....Let me sink lower still, that I may know the truth. Teach me to love again, to love life....Give me back my purity, the knowledge of the Mysteries, that I have betrayed and lost....Let me be truly lonely, that I may honestly pray."[3]

His prayer is not consistent. The Janus-like quality of his prayer that seeks rapprochement with Yvonne in one breath and in the other, he, like the Keats of *Ode to a Nightingale*,

1. Lowry, Malcolm: *Under the Volcano*, p. 145.
2. *Ibid.*, pp. 288-9.
3. *Ibid.*, p. 289.

feels forlorn and is brought back to his sole self. This preoccupation with the self is acidia in the religious sense. Lowry deepens the significance of spiritual ailment by beginning his novel with an epigraph from Bunyan. The epigraph from Bunyan's *Grace Abounding for the Chief of Sinners* in a nutshell gives the theme of the novel that consists in a sinner's inability to make prayer for the deliverance of his soul.

The sinner knows that his soul has been battered by worldly temptations and in the anguish of spirit he finds in him a craving for a respite from the nightmarish experience of being persecuted by conscience. But the difficulty with him is that despite all his yearning for the ineffable he finds himself sliding into hell. The excruciating pain arising from this vacilliation is reminiscent of T.S. Eliot in *Ash-Wednesday*.

> "For children at the gate
> Who will not go away and cannot pray:"[1]

Geoffrey embodies this dichotomy of human spirit, when he feels the necessity of the abounding love taming infernal powers that tempt him to damnation but the irony of his life is such that he feels himself utterly lost and beyond redemption. Geoffrey is so guilty of dust and sin that he despairingly utters: "Look up at that niche in the wall over there on the house where Christ is still, suffering, who would help you if you asked him: you cannot ask him."[2] Like Bunyan, Lowry deals with the theme of a sinner who feels that he has been cast off by God and there is no way out but to submit to despair. Geoffrey says, "God has little patience with remorse!"[3] The theme of guilt the novel deals with has a Calvinistic ring about it. The Calvinist doctrine of predestination accounts for fatalism in Geoffrey. He feels that he is a reprobate and there is something preordained about him. He finds himself led by some diabolical power which hovers over the novel: "...it struck him that some reckless murderous power was

1. *Selected Poems*, p. 91.
2. Lowry, Malcolm: *Under the Volcano*, p. 65.
3. *Ibid.*, p. 79.

drawing him on, forcing him, while he yet remained passionately aware of the all too possible consequences and somehow as innocently unconscious, to do without precaution or conscience what he would never be able to undo or gainsay, leading him irresistibly out..."[1]

Allied with this theme of Calvinist guilt is another primal theme of man's original sin in the garden of Eden and consequent expulsion from the Garden. When Geoffrey and Yvonne after their marriage in 1936 start living as a couple, they have a well tended garden. The well kept garden is symbolic of harmony and concerned of life but after Geoffrey's estrangement from Yvonne the garden is full of scum and rank weeds: "The tragedy, proclaimed, as they made their way up the crescent of the drive, no less by the gaping potholes in it than by the tall exotic plants, livid and crepuscular through his dark glasses, perishing on every hand of unnecessary thirst, staggering, it almost appeared, against one another, yet struggling like dying voluptuaries in a vision to maintain some final attitude of potency, or of a collective desolate fecundity,..."[2]

But the garden of his neighbour Mr. Quincey is well kept and the sign that admonishes a trespasser that he will face eviction, if he intends to despoil the beauty of the garden. But Geoffrey does not heed the warning and he makes a wreck of the garden and for having despoiled the garden his death is presided over by the Chief of Gardens at the end of the novel.

The novel has also the theme of sexual jealousy, the greeeyed monster, feeding on Geoffrey and pushing him into the abyss of horror. It speaks of the generosity of Yvonne that she comes back to Geoffrey with the noble mission of reconciling themselves and launching a life of love and affection. It appears that she has come to play the role of the Samaritan applying balm to the lacerated soul of Geoffrey. But Lowry's treatment of Yvonne's home-coming is ironic. It is ridiculous that the Samaritan is in the guise of Judas. Hugh, the half-brother of Geoffrey, is not a sole Judas betraying the trust

1. *Ibid*, p. 348.
2. *Ibid*, p 65.

of father-like Geoffrey by cuckolding him with Yvonne. Yvonne too relishes company with Hugh and on the Day of the Dead most of the time is away from Geoffrey for whose sake she has come over to Mexico and slakes her thirst for sensual appetite by swimming the pool with Hugh. Geoffrey's apprehension is not unfounded that Yvonne's relations with Hugh are shady.

He is fully aware of the deceitful nature of Yvonne's love for him and he gives vent to his pent-up fury: "Stay where you bloody are," ordered the Consul. "Of course I see the romantic predicament you two are in. But even if Hugh makes the most of it again it won't be long, it won't be long, before he realises he's only one of the hundred or so other ninney-hammers with gills like codfish and veins like racehorses—prime as goats all of them, hot as monkeys, salt as wolves in pride! No, one will be enough..."[1]

Sexual jealousy has unhinged Geoffrey and he finds that this traumatic experience knocks the bottom out of the gesture of Yvonne, the Samaritan: "What an uncommon time you two must have had, paddling palms and playing bubbies and titties all day under cover of saving me...Jesus. Poor little defenceless me—I hadn't thought of that."[2] The analogy to Othello's mind ravaged by sexual jealousy is obvious. Hugh first cuckolded Geoffrey in Paris and he has come again to Mexico to seduce Yvonne whom, Douglas Day with not enough justificaticn, calls 'the eternal feminine'.[3] Salon Ofelia where Geoffrey makes up his mind to snap all connections with Yvonne in the garb of a saviour recalls to mind the canker of sexual jealousy eating bit by bit the vitals of Hamlet. It has the frightful insinuation of Gertrude in adulterous relationship with Claudio. The theme of lust and sexual jealousy is a preoccupation of the poets of the thirties, the chief examplar of which is T.S. Eliot in *Sweeney among the Nightingales*:

1. *Ibid.*, p. 313.
2. *Ibid*, p. 313.
3. *Malcolm Lowry: A Biography*, p. 339.

"She and the lady in the cape
Are suspect, thought to be in league;
Therefore the man with heavy eyes
Declines the gambit, shows fatigue"[1]

Apart from the dominant strain of the tyranny of self that sets Geoffrey adrift in the sanctuary of despair, we find the political theme of the Spanish Civil War moving disturbingly through *Under the Volcano* 'like a conscience'.[2] 'They are losing the Battle of the Ebro'[3] runs like a refrain in the novel. The Spanish Civil War is a battle between the Republican Government of Spain and the Fascist forces under the leadership of General Franco in the thirties. The Republican Government receives help from the USSR and the Fascists are being helped by Germany and Italy. The Spanish Civil War has the catastrophic consequence of dividing Europe into two Camps. In 1938 the Republican Government crumbles and General Franco assumes power. Geoffrey's half-brother Hugh is a supporter of the Loyalists fighting the Fascist forces. He is a mild Marxman and proclaims that he will be going to Spain with a ship laden with explosives in support of the Loyalists.

But Geoffrey takes a dislike to a man with ideas like Hugh. To him there is nothing to choose between a Socialist or a Fascist or a Nazi and his rejoinder to Hugh, an ardent advocate of the Socialist system, has a chilling effect on him that all systems are bent on swallowing live struggling men and women. Geoffrey has no faith in the politics of commitment, because his concern is with the fundamentals of life. He wants to come to terms with the inscrutable power that tends to bring about a death of civilization: "Countries, civilizations, empires, great hordes, perish for no reason at all, and their soul and meaning with them...."[4]

1. *Selected Poems*, p. 47.
2. Introduction to *Under the Volcano*, p. xxii.
3. Lowry, Malcolm: *Under the Volcano*, p. 151.
4. *Ibid*., p. 310.

The ascendency of the Fascists in Spain is not an isolated phenomenon. It spreads to Mexico and organises the Fascist organisation of Union Militar tending to undermine the leftist, proletarian and agrarian character of the Republican Government of Cardenas in the thirties. The Fascists are in league with the Capitalists and make onslaughts on the Republican Mexican Government. The Mexican history of the late thirties is tragic, because there is a savage warfare between the leftists and rightists forces. Juan Cerillo's account of the barbarous regime after the death of Juarez sends shivers down the spine: "It was a country of slavery, where human beings were sold like cattle, and its native peoples, the Yaquis, the Papagos, the Tomasachics exterminated through deportation, or reduced to worse than penoage, their lands in thrall or in the hands of foreigners."[1] Juan himself, a bonafide slave, aged seven, has seen an older brother beaten to death, and another, bought for forty-five pesos, starved to death, later in the revolution, his mother was murdered. It is a heart-rending account of a character who has participated in the revolution.

It appears that the Spanish Civil War and the tragic history of Mexico during the reign of Mexmillian and Cardenas is likely to give the novel the air of a political tract but Heilman rightly feels that "the author does succeed in keeping the political phenomena on the periphery of the spiritual substance keeping them symbolic, using them for dramatic amplification of his metaphysic."[2] It is the 'Pelado' episode that unifies the political material and wrings the spiritual import out of it.

The word 'Pelado' is ambiguous. It means a shoeless illiterate. According to the Consul, "Pclados were indeed 'peeled one', the stripped, but also those who did not have to be rich to prey on the really poor. For instance those half breed petty politicians who will, in order to get into office just for one year, in which year they hope to put by enough to forswear work the rest of their lives, do literally anything

1 *Ibid*, p. 108.

2. The Sewance Review, Vol. LV (1947), p. 491.

whatsoever, from shining shoes, to acting as one who was not an 'aerial pigeon'."[1] It was perhaps one of those words that came with the Spaniards meaning either a thief or an exploiter.

Geoffrey, Yvonne and Hugh find themselves in the company of a Pelado, perhaps a Spaniard, in a bus on way to Tomalin. The Pelado gets down from the bus and robs an Indian dying beside the road of his money. He pays the bus fare with the stolen money and swaggers into a pulqueria, stepping high with a fatuous smile of triumph on his face. It shows the cruelty and inhumanity not only of an individual but a civilization at a particular historical moment spawning a race with a fiendish character.

The heartless character of the civilization consists not only in an individual robbing a man on the point of death of his money but the attitude of all passengers standing passive and listless, when an Indian is struggling with life in the hedge. Yvonne gives a nervous cry and turns on her heel and says, "It's just that I can't stand the sight of blood, damn it."[2] The Consul seemed lost in reflection and said sharply, "You can't touch him—it's the law",[3] when Hugh made an attempt to do something for the dying Indian. The Consul reminded Hugh that if he did something for the dying Indian, he might become an accessory after the fact and all were lost in a futile controversy whether it was a case of robbery or attempted murder.

In was a pathetic sight that the chest of the Indian heaved like a spent swimmer's, his stomach contracted and dilated rapidly, but all were bystanders frittering time in a hair-splitting analysis of the causes leading to the death of the Indian. It is shirking the sacred responsibility of doing good to a man dying: "...there was no limit to their ingenuity. Though the most potent and final obstacle to doing anything about the Indian was this discovery that it was not one's business but

1. Lowry, Malcolm: *Under the Volcano*, p. 235.
2. *Ibid.*, p. 242.
3. *Ibid.*, p. 243.

some one else's."[1] It is nothing but dehumanisation robbing people of their essential character. It is sheer callousness that takes pity away from man, the impulse to approach, and terror, the impulse to escape and reconciles them by prudence, "the conviction it is better to stay where you are".[2] It is a atomisation, sundering a man's relation with the community and shoving him into the cave of his mind.

Thus, the political reality that makes non-intervention a cherished policy in international relations at the time of the Spanish Civil War is nothing but a manifestation of the spiritual apathy of man. Hugh, with all his protestations of commitment to the Marxist ideology, is by and large moving in the realm of ideas and he himself admits that when the Battle of the Ebro is lost, he is away from Spain. It is nothing but evasion of responsibility and obession with one's own self. Heilman cogently argues, "It is above all the story of a good Samaritan—only there is no Samaritan...(Geoffrey's Ship, a gun boat disguised as merchantman had been named the 'Samaritan', a comment upon modern Samaratinism)."[3]

Against this backdrop of indifference and nonchalance that leads to the death of Geoffrey at the hands of Fascist forces in Chapter Twelve of the novel, we find the novelist striving hard to develop the theme of Goethe's Faust stated in one of the epigraphs with which the novel begins: "Whosoever unceasingly strives upward... him can we save."[4] Though Geoffrey flees all contact with Yvonne at Salon Ofelia racing into the Malebolge, the eighth circle of Dante's Inferno, in the direction of the Farolito saying. "I've been beguiled by your offers of a sober and non-alcoholic Paradise....But now I've made up my melodramatic little mind ... I love hell, I can't wait to get back there. In fact I'm running."[5]

It does not mean that Geoffrey is claimed by infernal powers. He, no doubt, is prone to diabolical powers but

1. *Ibld.*, p. 245.
2. *Ibid.*, p. 249.
3. The Sewance Review, Vol. LV (1947), p. 489.
4. Lowry, Malcolm: *Under the Volcano*, p. 2.
5. *Ibid.*, pp. 313-4.

Goethe's theme in Faust that 'whosoever unceasingly strives upward...him can we save' also informs his being, though its voice is muted and muffled. In Chapter Nine Geoffrey conceives of an arcadia to which he will repair along with Yvonne: "They would buy all their food, just as Hugh said, from a store beyond the woods, and see no body, save a few fishermen whose white boats in winter they would see pitching at anchor in the bay. She would cook and clean and Geoffrey would chop the wood and bring water from the well....They would continue to live, in simplicity and love, in their home between the forest and the sea."[1] *Under the Volcano*, the Inferno of a contemplated trilogy, is redeemed fitfully by the vision of Paradise recreated in his *October Ferry to Gabriola*. In *Under the Volcano*, "a book about heaven and hell and the necessity of choice between them,"[2] there is no gainsaying that the protagonist is overwhelmed with infernal powers but Geoffrey Firmin is a "giant character whose sloth or acidia ironically suggests the Promethean rebel whose total alienation from life etches the desired opposite, whose inability to love defines what love is."[3]

Geoffrey's despair is religious. This despair is an attribute of many religious poets such as John Donne. In *Hymn to God the Father*, John Donne craves the grace of God because he feels greatly ashamed of his wallowing in sins. He knows that the grace of God abounds and he will have God's grace but his ways are so sinful that he will again relapse from God's grace into the quicksand of evil passions. The ambivalence which marks a religious poet such as John Donne is also true in some measure of Geoffrey in *Under the Volcano*. Geoffrey is profoundly ambivalent in his prayers as Ethen is by and large in *October Ferry to Gabriola*. Geoffrey wants to have the purity, the knowledge of the Mysteries he has betrayed and lost in one breath and in another breath he wants to be left alone. This ambivalence is syntactically poised in a

1. *Ibid.*, p. 271.
2. Burgess Anthony: *Spectator*, Jan. 20, 1957, p. 74.
3. *Ibid.*, p. 74.

number of passages scattered all over the novel and gives richness to Geoffrey's character.

(B) ART OF CHARACTERISATION

Though Lowry writes a long exegesis in defence of *Under the Volcano*, he makes a few concessions to Cape's reader. He agrees that the reader's criticism of the weakness of character-drawing is valid. He admits that character-drawing is "not only weak but virtually non-existent, save with certain minor characters."[1] Characterisation is non-existent in the traditional sense of the creation of static characters. In recent times, as a result of increased speculation into the nature of states of consciousness, writers have become disstisfied with the traditional method of character-creation.

It is realised that a psychologically accurate account of what a man is at any given moment can be had neither in terms of a static description of his character nor in terms of a group of chronologically arranged reactions to a series of circumstances. They have become interested in those aspects of consciousness which cannot be viewed as a progression of individual and self-existing moments but which are essentially dynamic rather than static in nature. The present moment is specious. It denotes the ever fluid passing of 'the already' into the 'not yet' and therefore retrospect and anticipation constitute the very essence of consciousness at any specified time.

In the light of an epistemology conceiving of the psyche of man in a state of perpetual flux, a static character sketch becomes an arbitrary formalization of real facts and this awareness in Lowry prompts him to devise a fluid technique which will enable him to utilize constantly those ever present contacts with the past which constitute the very stuff of consciousness. Thus, when Lowry states that characterization is virtually non-existent, he perhaps echoes D.H. Lawrence who in one of his letters wishes to demolish the notion of the old stable ego and aims at recreating changes in the character

1. Quoted by Douglas Day: *Malcolm Lowry: A Biography*, p. 318.

through all allotropic states. Characterization is there but it is in conformity with the new conception of character existing from moment to moment blending memory and desire. And hence Lowry says, "There are a thousand writers who can draw adequate characters till all is blue for one who can tell you anything new about hell fire. And I am telling you something new about hell fire."[1]

A novel about hell fire is embodied in terms of the interaction of a number of individual characters, despite Lowry's statement that the four main characters are not individuals any way, but "aspects of the same man, or of the human spirit."[2] If we go by what the novelist says about his characters, *Under the Volcano* becomes a schematic allegorical novel. The novel, no doubt, has an allegorical import but characters retain their individuality and merit a consideration of their individual lives contributing to the development of the theme of perdition consuming the life of its protagonist.

We can divide characters in *Under the Volcano* into four categories. The first category comprises Geoffrey Firmin, the British Consul, and his wife Yvonne in the Mexican town of Quauhnahuac. The second group is composed of Jacques, a playmate of Geoffrey, at Leaswoe and a French film producer who has been living in Quauhnahuac for four years and Hugh, a half-brother of Geoffrey, who comes to Quauhnahuac a few days before Yvonne reaches there to renew her marriage with Geoffrey. The third group is made up of Dr. Vigil treating neurosis and sexual disorder, Sr. Bustament the manager of a cinema house, Mr. Quincey an American farmer and a neighbour of Geoffrey and Cantina owners like Cervantes. Characters of this group are sympathetic to Geoffrey. The fourth group is made up of fascists attached to their organisation Union Militar at Parian in Mexico. Characters of this group remain anonymous and are not endowed with individuality. One is called the Chief of Municipality, the other the Chief of Rostrums and the third the Chief of Gardens. The person who runs the Farolilo, a Cantina at

1. Day, Douglas: *Malcolm Lowry: A Biography*, p. 318.
2. *Ibid.*, p. 3;9.

Parian, is Diasdado, also called the Elephant and his son a Few Fleas. Characters of this group are poised against Geoffrey, keep surveillance on him, plot against him and make away with his life. These four groups of characters act upon one another and develop the theme of the novel.

But unless we take into account Mexico, its landscape and its history and how they interact with the human drama enacted by the above-mentioned groups of characters the novel remains bereft of its significance. About Mexico what Lowry says is germane to our discussion of the art of characterization: "There was no denying its beauty, fatal or cleansing as it happened to be, the beauty of the Earthly Paradise itself."[1] M. Laurelle's description of Quauhnahuac, the locale of the novel, is pregnant with serious import: "Quauhnahuac was like the times in this respect, wherever you turned the abyss was waiting for you round the corner Dormitory for vultures and city Moloch! When Christ was being crucified, so ran the sea-borne, hieratic legend, the earth had opened all through this country, though the coincidence could hardly have impressed anyone then!"[2] The part played by the ponderous and melancholy Mexican landscape is reminiscent of Wessex in the novels of Hardy. Thus, apart from a study of human characters, an analysis of the Mexican landscape that looms large in the consciousness of the characters becomes imperative.

Under the Volcano is the tale of Geoffrey Firmin's moral disintegration and his death at the hands of fascists on the Day of the Dead in November 1938. The novel tells us how on the Day of the Dead Geoffrey starts boozing at Bellavista bar at dawn, when Yvonne comes there for making up quarrel with him. He keeps on moving from Cantina to Cantina drinking to his fill and ultimately disdainfully turns down the proferred hands of love by Yvonne. It is intriguing that Geoffrey, who, in his unsent epistle after Yvonne divorces him, looks upon her as his saviour but contemptuously breaks off his connections with her and rushes towards Parian, the

1. Lowry, Malcolm: *Under the Volcano*, p. 10.
2. *Ibid.*, pp. 15-16.

centre of fascist activists. This impulse to self-annihilation finds an explanation in the scattered bits of information the novelist offers us about Geoffrey's parentage and his boyhood. We can piece together these fragments and build up a coherent picture of the man who destroys himself.

Geoffrey's mother dies, when he is a child in Kashmir. Within a year or so his father marries again and after begetting a child, named Hugh, disappears. It is said about his father that he flees north off Srinagar in search of Himavat, impelled by some religious frenzy. He vanishes, leaving Geoffrey, at Srinagar with his half-brother Hugh then a baby in arms, and his step-mother. The step-mother dies too, leaving the two children alone in India. After the sudden disappearance of his father, the death of his mother and step-mother, Geoffrey along with Hugh comes to England to be raised by collateral relatives. Geoffrey comes to stay with "the family of the famous English poet, Abraham Taskerson."[1] When Geoffrey comes to his foster parent, Abraham Taskerson, he appears to be 'a broody creature of fifteen, so shy and yet so curiously self-contained, who wrote poetry that old Taskerson (who'd stay at home) apparently encouraged him with, and who sometimes burst out crying if you mentioned in his presence the word "father" or "mother".[2]

This gives us an account of an 'Anglo-Indian orphan'[3] suffering acutely from a sense of emotional abandonment, because his father has disappeared and his mother has died. The absence of parents has left a void in him making him secretive and pensive. This sullen and introspective boy of fifteen finds himself in the boisterous company of the sons of Abraham Taskerson. The sons of Taskerson are "unprecedented, portentous, drinkers",[4] though none is above school age. In their house the pantry was always bulging with barrels of beer to be tapped by anyone who did. In a mere five-mile walk Taskerson's sons stop at as many pubs and drink a pint

1. *Ibid* , p. 16.
2. *Ibid.*, p. 16.
3. *Ibid.*, p. 16.
4. *Ibid.*, p. 18.

or two of powerful beer in each. Even the youngest, who had not turned fifteen would get through his six pints in an afternoon. But Geoffrey who was called the Old Bean "sat bashful and out of place, his glass of pale bitter untouched, shylv trying to make conversation with Mr. Taskerson."[1] Geoffrey disliked the taste of beer and his "nose was always in a book."[2] He finds himself out of tune with the bohemian sons of Taskerson but he finds there a French boy of his age, Jacques Laruelle.

Jacques felt oddly attracted to Geoffrey and saw a great deal of him Jacques and Geoffrey go into the town full of laughing pretty girls and do yachting on a marine lake. Though initially Geoffrey is reluctant to immerse himself in the wanton revelry of Taskerson's sons, he starts overcoming shyness. With Jacques he too goes about picking up girls: "... The Old Bean, who was a virgin to put it mildly, and Jacques, who pretended he was not, fell into the habit of picking up girls on the promenade, walking to the golf course, separating there, and meeting later."[3] On one of these nocturnal excursions Jacques and his girl discover Geoffrey and another girl in the notorious 'Hell Bunker' on the eighth fairway. After embarrassed readjustment, of clothing the four proceed to an inn 'The case is Altered', for a drink, and are refused by the proprietor of the ground on their minority. After that incident of love in an abyss and discovery, the relations between Geoffrey and Jacques deteriorate and they go their separate ways, Geoffrey to school and spectacular exploits as commander of a Boat in World War I both decorated and court-martialled and Jacques to film-making. Since then they meet in Quauhnahuac after two decades, Geoffrey at the end of a long consular service in various parts of the world and Jacques retired from film-making.

The incident that takes place on S.S. Samaritan fills him with a sense of guilt. Q-Boat under the Command of Geoffrey captures the crew of a German Submarine and consigns them

1. *Ibid.*, p. 19.
2. *Ibid.*, p. 19.
3. *Ibid.*, p. 21.

to flames in the furnace of S.S. Samaritan. This guilt of the German crew consumed by flames in the presence of the stokers and other crewmen rankles in his mind: "It was only once or twice during those later months when drunk that to M. Laruelle's astonishment he suddenly began proclaiming not only his guilt in the matter but that held always suffered horribly on account of it. He went much further. No blame attached to the stokers. No question arose of any order given them. Flexing his muscles he ardonically announced the single-handed accomplishment himself of the deed."[1]

But Daniel B. Dodson questions the veracity of Geoffrey's complicity in the crime and cites Geoffrey's involvement in the killing of the German crew in the furnace as an example of Lowry's carelessness in respect of details. He observes, "At the beginning of World War I,...he would have been seventeen, and at the end in 1918, twenty-one, an impossibly tender age to have been commander of a gunboat."[2] It is not an improbability in the light of intense hatred towards the Germans. The atmosphere during the war is charged with strong passions on both sides and the outrageous killing of the German crew is not out of keeping with spite and venom vitiating relations between nations and "...it was easy to think of the Consul as a kind of lachrymose pseudo "Lord Jim" living in a self-imposed exile, brooding, despite his award, over his lost honour, his secret, and imagining that a stigma would cline to him because of it throughout his whole life."[3] The analogy to Lord Jim is obvious but Jim spends the rest of his brief life attempting to atone for a moment of instinctive cowardice, while the Consul's career is marked by progressive degeneration.

The causes of his degeneration lie buried in the biographical snatches of Geoffrey, a castaway, cut off from filial love. His sense of loneliness is exacerbated by his gnawing guilt over the German crewmen roasted alive in the furnace of boat under his stewardship. From his childhood

1. *Ibid.*, p 33.
2. *Malcolm Lowry*, p. 25.
3. Lowry, Malcolm: *Under the Volcano*, p. 33.

the Consul has had a fatalistic distrust of the possibility of any one's understanding devotion to him. He has not experienced love since he is a kid and in his conversation with Hugh he finds the universe bleak and awful: "Your mother, my step-mother died, all those dreadful things seeming to happen at once as though the in-laws of catastrophe had suddenly arrived from nowhere, or, perhaps, Damchock, and moved in on us..."[1]

In 1935 he meets Yvonne Constable in Granada. They marry and lead a life of felicity for perhaps a year. Geoffrey very sensitively recaptures the felicity of their marital life in the first year, "For ho, Yvonne, I am so haunted continuously by the thought of your songs, of your warmth and merriment, of your simplicity and comradeship, of your abilities in a hundred ways, your fundamental sanity, your untidiness, your equally excessive neatness—the sweet beginnings of our marriage."[2] If Dana Hilliot, the protagonist in Lowry's *Ultramarine*, is a fictional analogue for the author himself, Geoffrey, too, in much more complicated ways mirrors the author. The breakdown of Lowry's first marriage in late 1937, when they are in Mexico and his subsequent drunks, find a parallel to Geoffrey's breakdown of marriage to Yvonne, his subsequent indulgence in drinking bouts. His marriage with Yvonne fell apart, by the time Hugh his half-brother met them in Paris in 1936. Geoffrey had become drunk and Hugh does not help matters by sleeping with the distraught Yvonne.

Geoffrey feels that the sacrament of marriage has been defiled and this puts him out. His resentment is less towards Hugh and more towards Yvonne: "Clear that I forgive you, as somehow I have never wholly been able to forgive Yvonne."[3] But Hugh is not less culpable, because his flirtation with Yvonne drives a wedge between Geoffrey and Yvonne, and the yawning gulf proves to be the cause of his undoing. Geoffrey says to Hugh, "...before that day what you did impulsively and have tried to forget in the cruel abstraction of

1. *Ibid.*, p. 78.
2. *Ibid.*, p. 39.
3. *Ibid.*, pp. 77-8.

youth will begin to strike you in a new and darker light. I am afraid that you may indeed, precisely because you are a good and simple person at bottom and genuinely respect more than most the principles and decencies that might have prevented it, fall hair, as you grow older and your conscience less robust, to a suffering on account of it more abominable than any you have caused me. How may I help you? How ward it off? How shall the murdered man convince his assassin he will not haunt him."[1]

The canker of sexual jealousy, that creeps into Geoffrey, when Hugh starts philandering with his wife Yvonne, fills Geoffrey with agony. The anguish in his soul accentuates, when he finds Hugh in the Mexican town of Quauhnahuac. Geoffrey calls Hugh, "...my-little-snake-in the grass my-little-anguish-in-herba."[2] If Geoffrey looks upon Hugh as an agent that disrupts harmony with Yvonne, there is no substance in the argument that Hugh is a part of Geoffrey himself.

Hugh is an antithesis of Geoffrey. From the little biographical snatch of Geoffrey's life in the novel we learn that Geoffrey during his stay with the English poet Abraham Taskerson composed poems and this is in support of the thesis I would like to develop that he has the sensibility of a poet, a poet in the line of Baudelaire and Rimbaud. He is tempted, no doubt, by infernal powers, he does not have the pretensions of Hugh who wants to transform the world by his ideas but all his schemes of a new social order remain wish-fulfilment: "For Hugh, at twentynine, still dreamed, even then, of changing the world (there was no other way of saying this) through his actions—just as Laruelle, at forty-two, had still then not quite given up hope of changing it through the great films he proposed somehow to make. But today these dreams seemed absurd and presumptuous."[3]

Hugh, who receives the affection of a father from Geoffrey, does not suffer from any qualm of conscience in betraying him by seducing Vvonne who has come to redeem Geoffrey from

1. *Ibid.*, p. 78-9.
2. *Ibid.*, p. 134.
3. *Ibid*, p. 9.

wreck. Hugh also does not shrink from ravishing the wife of Bolowski, the publisher of his songs. He has the readiness to forgo moral scruples, when they become an impediment in his way to success. In his journalistic career he first strikes an 'anti-semitic stance': "a form of private anti-semitism became part of his life. He sweated racial hatred in the night. In his day-dreams he became the instigator of pogroms a'l inclusive and hence, bloodless,"[1] but after sometime he becomes a semitophile: "were not...the Jews themselves cast out, exploited, and wandering of the earth, even as they, even, once, as he."[2]

He volubly speaks of his support to the cause of the Spainish Republicans but it is a mere lip service to an ideal. He does not dedicate himself to the realization of Marxist ideas dear to his heart. His much-vaunted talk about a journey by Sea with explosives in support of the Loyalists remains a mere talk, because the novel does not tell us that Hugh reaches Spain with his reinforcement. Our last encounter with Hugh in the novel is in a forest near Parian singing Loyalist songs. He is perhaps a rolling stone that gathers no moss.

He shows fervour and zeal but lacks consistency and perseverance to give a shape to his ideas. This irresolution and vacillation is the very principle of his life: When he advances with a view to doing good to a dying Indian in the hedge, Geoffrey reminds him of the Mexican Law that makes a man lending helping hand to a dying man an accessory after the fact. He recoils and leaves the Indian gasping for breath. This is also a proof of the lack of tenacity in Hugh with which he should have pursued his political objectives.

The sole thing he is shown enamoured of is either a swim with Yvonne in a pool or a horse ride with Yvonne. He finds himself in his elements in the company of Yvonne and his fascination for her is irresistible: "Unconsciously, he had been watching her, her bare brown neck and arms, the yellow slacks, and the vivid scarlet flowers behind her, the brown hair

1. *Ibid* , p. 171.
2. *Ibid.*, p. 171.

circling her ears; the graceful swift movement of yellow sandles in which she seems to dance, to be floating rather than walking."[1] He wavers, when the question of a film adherence to political ideals comes, but he does not let slip the opportunity of flirting with Yvonne. Leaving Geoffrey with Laruelle in the house of the latter, Hugh and Yvonne set out for the Square.

It is this passionate involvement of Hugh in Yvonne that hastens Geoffrey's estrangement from Yvonne in spite of her desire to resolve the stalemates in her relations with the husband. Thus Hugh plays the part of precipitating a crisis in Geoffrey's marital life and is responsible in a large measure for Geoffrey's damnation. Geoffrey's perception of Hugh's essential nature is essentially apt: "What have you ever done for humanity, Hugh, with all your oratio obliqua about the capitalist system, except talk, and thrive on it, until your soul stinks."[2] When Hugh is off his guard, he becomes shamefully aware of the duplicity in his character. "You are a liar, said the trees tossing in the garden. You are a traitor, rattled the plantain leaves. And a coward too,..."[3]

In *Under the Volcano* Hugh is not a sole traitor that brings ruin to an essentially noble character Geoffrey. It is M. Laruelle who is another Judas betraying his friend Geoffrey with whom he has got association since boyhood with the intervening period of separation from him for two decades. M. Laruelle, born in Languion in the Moselle Country, is the son of a philatelist: "He is an elderly aesthete, a confirmedly promiscuous bachelor, with a rather unctuous possessive manner toward women."[4] He stays at Quauhnahuac for four years, almost five and he still feels 'like a wanderer on another planet'.[5] His Villa at Calle Nicargua is full of some collections of antique art. On the battlements of the mirador of

1. *Ibid.*, p. 98.
2. *Ibid.*, pp. 312-13.
3. *Ibid.*, p. 151.
4. *Ibid.*, p. 8.
5. *Ibid.*, p. 9.

his house are too billious looking angels. The angels, carved out of pink stone, kneel facing one another in profile against the sky, while behind sit solemnly two nameless objects like marzipan cannon balls.

It is a queer combination of angels and cannon balls. Inside the house are grisly Orozco charcoal drawings of an unexampled horrendousness snarl down from the walls. One of the terrible pictures relates to harpies grappling on a smashed bed-stead among broken bottles of tequila gnashing their teeth. There is another painting remotely under the influence of Michaelangelo. It is called "Los-Borrachones" portraying: "Down, headlong into hades, selfish and florid-faced, into a tumult of fire-spangled fiends, Medusae and belching monstrosities, with swallow dives, or awkwardly, with dread backward leaps, shrieking among falling bottles and emblems of broken hopes, plunged the drunkards; up, up, flying palely, selflessly into the light toward heaven, soaring sublimely in pairs, male sheltering female, shielded themselves by angels with abnegating wings, shot the sober."[1]

Though M. Laruelle is an aesthete collecting works of art, he shows no sign of imbibing anything from the picture of the drunkards and the sober just alluded to. Geoffrey drinks mescal and eyebrows are raised at him treating him as a debauch. He is a drunk but M. Laruelle, who is a connoisseur of art depicting the punishment that visits the drunks and the felicity that comes to the sober, is himself a drunk with the charm of Yvonne. A very revealing portrait of Laruelle has been done in Chapter Six by Hugh: "With sloping shoulders and handsome, rather swarthy features, though he was obviously a European, doubtless in some state of exile, was confronting them, and it was as though the whole of this man, by some curious fiction, reached up to the crown of his perpendicularly raised Panama hat, for the gap below seemed to Hugh still occupied by something, a sort of halo or spiritual property of his body, or the essence of some guilty secret perhaps that he kept under the hat but which

1. *Ibid.*, p. 199.

was now momentarily exposed, fluttering and embarrassed. He was confronting them, though smiling, it appeared, at Yvonne alone, his blue, bold protuberant eyes expressing an incredulous dismay, his black eyebrows frozen in a comedian's arch: he hesitated: then this man, who wore his coat open and trousers very high over a stomach they had probably been designed to conceal but merely succeeded in giving the character of an independent tumescence of the lower part of his body."[1]

Laruelle in his soliloquy tells us about the flame of love for Yvonne that burns in his heart in all its incandescences: "...what had reunited the Consul and himself for a time, even after Yvonne left, was not, on either side, remorse. It was perhaps, partly more the desire for that illusory comfort, about as satisfying as biting on an aching tooth, to be derived from the mutual unspoken pretence that Yvonne was still here."[2] Thus it is evident that Laruelle like Hugh feels distraught with the charm of Yvonne.

Beneath the charming exterior of Laruelle's aestheticism lurks the barbarian in him. When he wants to get a confirmation from Geoffrey of whether Yvonne has come for reconciliation or not, Geoffrey wonders at M. Laruelle peristently poking his nose into their affairs. He finds something shady about Laruelle's solicitude for Yvonne. He sees through the lascivious game of Laruelle and says to him: "Get it a little straighter still. You're thinking of youself."[3] He makes a scathing exposure of the hipocrisy of M. Laruelle: "But the abominable impact on his whole being at the moment of the fact that hideously elongated cucumiform bundle of blue nerves and gills below the steaming unselfconscious stomach had sought its pleasure in his wife's body brought him trembling to his feet. How loathsome, how incredibly loathsome was reality."[4] Thus Hugh and M. Laruelle are obsessed with inordinate passion for Yvonne and the sight of these two

1. *Ibid* , p. 190.
2. *Ibid.*, p. 13.
3. *Ibid.*, p. 121.
4. *Ibid.*, p. 207.

characters pursuing Yvonne arouses indignation and nausea in Geoffrey. His faith in life is shaken, when he finds himself in the midst of base passions getting the better of the mind of characters such as Hugh and Laruelle.

If we summarily reject Geoffrey as a character lost in the world of drinks, we do injustice to him. Stephen Spender aptly remarks: "Fundamentally *Under the Volcano* is no more about drinking than King Lear is about senility. It is about the Consul, which is another matter, for what we feel about him is that he is great and shattered."[1]

Forces, that shatter him, work through Laruelle and Hugh, they are the forces of vile passions. Geoffrey's malady is not physical as Dr. Vigil, who himself is a good drunk, says about Geoffrey, "Sickness is not only in body, but in that part used to be called: Soul. Poor your friends, he spend his money on earth in such continuous tragedies."[2] Geoffrey says to Yvonne, "I do love you. Only—" "I can never forgive you deeply enough."[3] But Yvonne's letter from America, posted just after her estrangement, reaches Geoffrey when she meets him on the Day of the Dead November 1938 and beseeches him, "I have put aside all my pride to beg your forgiveness, to offer you mine...For my life is irrevocably and forever bound to yours....What release can be compared to the release of love?—I am in your hands now. Save—"[4]

As Geoffrey has the experience of being bereaved of his father and mother since boyhood, Yvonne too has the sad experience of her mother's death, a troublesome life and her father, a Consul in Chile who is an alcoholic wreck. Yvonne is not only the outdoor girl of the Hawaiian island fond of swimming, golf, dancing. She is not only an expert equestrian and an actress at fourteen, and at fifteen, leading lady to Bill Hodson but she has also experienced the breakdown of her first marriage and the death of her first child. She is a woman who has known the meaning of love and tragedy and

1. Spender, Stephen: Introduction to *Under the Volcano*, p. IX.
2. Lowry, Malcolm: *Under the Volcano*, p. 5.
3. *Ibid.*, p. 197.
4. *Ibid.*, p. 367.

she is perfectly justified, when she says that Geoffrey knows little of her life stricken with terror: "How little he knew of this period of her life, of that terror, the terror, terror that still could wake her in the night from the recurrent nightmare of things collapsing."[1]

She is in need of love but Geoffrey's mind is tormented by doubt about her fidelity. He is so torn by a strife between the impulse to love and impulse to hate at Salon Ofelia, that he tears asunder his relation with Yvonne and on reaching the Farolito, clasps Maria, a prostitute. Though he forgoes the love of Yvonne for the sake of a whore, his moral conscience never deserts him even in this hour of wilful descent into inferno: "...Her body was nothing, an abstraction merely, a calamity, a fiendish apparatus for calamitous sickening sensation; it was disaster, it was the horror of waking up in the morning in Oaxaca, his body fully clothed, at half-past three, every morning after Yvonne had gone."[2] Geoffrey's amour with Maria is an eye-opener for him and enables him to distinguish the real from the illusory: "...God is it possible to suffer more than this, out of this suffering something must be born, and what would be born was his own death for ah, how alike are the groans of love to those of the dying, how alike, those of love, to those of the dying."[3]

Though Geoffrey has a desire for death and moves towards his ineluctable destruction, the voice of conscience never loses its resonance. "...for the conscience that rages underneath anew and is bursting one's heart burns so fiercely with the fires of hell a bar of red hot iron is as a mere chill to it."[4] Geoffrey's mind is akin to the mind of a tragic hero. The mind of a tragic hero is like a little kingdom that suffers the nature of an insurrection. The war is between the familiars, of the moral universe and passions that slumber in the unconscious and terrifies the mind of Geoffrey. Passions latent in the unconscious invade Geoffrey but Geoffrey refuses to be vanquished. It is only the insidious power of a flourishing

1. *Ibid* , p. 260.
2. *Ibid* , p. 349.
3. *Ibid* , p. 349.
4. *Ibid.*, p. 350.

and corrupt political force represented by fascists that not only kills Geoffrey but the innocent and defenceless indigenous Mexican population of which the Indian that dies under the hedge is a specimen.

Characters with loyalty to the political ideology of fascists work like a ruthless apparatus. They make Geoffrey a captive and charges him with being a pelado, a Bolshevik and a member of the International Brigade. Geoffrey, though a good deal battered by the conflict between the families and the infernal powers, refuses to acquiesce to fascist forces that exalt the irrational in man. He strikes the Chief of Rostrums and hurls legitimate accusations on his tribe: "You poxboxes. You Coxcoxes. You killed that Indian. You tried to kill him and make it look like an accident.... Give me my papersback."[1] This shows that Geoffrey's will is indomitable and does not break under the severest strain, even when he is shot dead and thrown into the ravine.

Anthony Burgess's portrait reveals Geoffrey's essential nature, "...He contains within himself a picture gallery of all the tragic heroes, from Oedipus Tyrannus and Philoctetes (the names of two ships in the novel) to Faust and Hamlet, is a fresh tragic creation in his own right, since he is a product of our own period. His situation is hopeless, but he does not whine: he even maintains a courtesy proper to his rank. He does not lie in bed like Oblomov, waiting for the end of a regime; he drinks steadily and, through the drink, achieves poet's or saint's clairvoyance. He knows precisely what is going on. The attainment of self-knowledge, however cut off from the ability to act, is seen to be an aspect of the heroic."[2]

(C) TECHNIQUE

In his letters Malcolm Lowry makes it clear that he is in rebellion against the realist novel: "unquestionably what one is after is a new form, a new approach to reality itself."[3]

1. *Ibid*, pp. 371-72.
2. *Spectator*, Jan. 20, 1967, p. 74.
3. Quoted in *The Art of Malcolm Lowry*, edited by Anne Smith, p. 97.

This rebellion of Lowry against the realist school in fiction is also voiced by Ethan in *October Ferry to Gabriola*: "A novelist presents a less of life the more closely he approaches what he thinks of as his realism."[1] Lowry's aesthetic position and his technique owes much to Expressionism that ignores the external reality and lays emphasis on the passionate expression or the inner reality. To an Expressionist, reality resides primarily in the mind of the perceiver, not in the objective world. Lowry, who had some knowledge of and considerable interest in expressionist painting, theatre, music and film, believes that reality is dynamic and perpetually protean. A picture of reality that is perpetually new finds a better medium in poetry than in prose.

Though Lowry's medium in *Under the Volcano* is prose, he writes poetry: "It is that the author's equipment, such as it is subjective rather than objective, a better equipment, in short, for a certain kind of poet than a novelist."[2] To Lowry the conception of *Under the Volcano* is essentially poetic because "he saw that the novel-form's only hope of survival lay in its being taken over by poets"[3] Unless a reader is responsive to the poetic organisation of the novel, he is prone to agree with the Cape reader that the book is much too long and over elaborate for its content, and could have been more effective, if some of its bulk would have been excised. Thus we have to bear in mind that the conception is poetic rather than novelistic.

As the meaning of a good poem comes to a reader after several readings, I agree with Lowry that the full meaning will reveal itself, explode in the mind, after repeated readings. It is not pretentious on Lowry's part to expect several readings of the reader. If we recall James Joyce's assertion that he had taken eighteen years to write *Finnegan's Wake*, he saw no reason why it should not take eighteen years to read.

The poetic organisation of *Under the Volcano* becomes evident because once, we are into the story, we are less aware

1. *Ibid*., p. 111.
2. Quoted in Douglas Day's *Malcolm Lowry: A Biography*, p. 318.
3. Burgess, Anthony: *Spectator*, Jan. 20, 1967, p. 74.

of the realistic side of the story than of the imaginative richness. Heilman's remark is apt: "The minds of the characters are sensitive recording instruments, tenacious alike of the facts and of their suggestive value. The book is a cornucopia of image; both the psychic and the outer worlds have a tangibility which a thoughtless slice of realism could never produce; humour and horror are never alleged but are moulded into a hard and yet resilient narrative substance. But one is always driven to seek out the evocation that trail off behind the facts."[1]

Under the Volcano abounds in the evocation that hangs about the facts. Apart from the immediate level of the story on which Bale Edmonds lays emphasis, "We are always aware of a multitude of suggestions which, in their continual impingement upon us, reminds us of recurrent images of Shakespeare."[2] A recurrent Shakespearean image plays a considerable part in making dramatic texture coherent as well as intricate. The same motif which was touched upon in the first act, through the imagery, is taken up again in the second; it undergoes a fuller execution and expansion, perhaps in the third and fourth. The leitmotifs of imagery bind the separate elements of the play together into a real organic structure. In *Under the Volcano* Malcolm Lowry takes recourse to this recurrent motif that unifies diverse materials into a unity.

The action takes place in November on the Day of the Dead. Geoffrey feels that his soul is dying. His soul appears to him a town ravaged and stricken. There is a reference to an imaginary town by the sea that burns up. The death imagery relates to a funeral, the burial customs and to a refrain in Second Chapter "A corpse will be transported by express!"[3] and to the death of Yvonnes's child from her first husband. Geoffrey imagines a man lying dead near his swimming pool, he recalls Dr. Faustus's death, encounters a dying Indian under the hedge, when he is on way to Tomalin. There

1. *The Sewance Review*, Vol. LV, 1947, p. 488.

2. *Ibid.*, p. 488.

3. Lowry, Malcolm: *Under the Volcano*, p. 43.

is a reference to a Cantina La Sepultra, suggestive of death. Always there are vultures, pariah dogs, the noise of target practice. The novel begins with the desolate splendour that pervades the Hotel Casinodelaselva haunted by the ghosts of ruined gamblers and in whose magnificent Olympic pool no one swims and whose jai-alai courts are grass-grown and deserted and the spring-boards stand empty and mournful. Reference is there to the ruin of the Maximilian palace which 'seemed part of a nightmare'[1] and where ghosts were quarrelling: "No, you loved yourself, you loved your misery more than I. You did this deliberately to us." "I"?[2] Frustrations and failures are everywhere—engagements are missed, the light fails in a cinema.

Always we are reminded of the barranca, or ravine, near the town, a horrendous abyss. The barranca becomes Dante's the Malebolge, the eighth ring of the Inferno: "The Malebolge was the barranca, the ravine which wound through the country. . .".[3] There are various allusions to Dante's inferno and Dr. Vigil perhaps faintly reminds Virgil in the role of a guide to Consul's Dante. Geoffrey feels he is in hell, and quotes Donne on sin and defiantly says at Salon Ofelia 'I love hell'. There are four hundred pools of water at Quauhnahuac and Geoffrey fails to appease his thirst. Marvell's line from Clorinda and Daimon: "Might a soul bathe there and be clean or slake its drought?"[4] runs like a refrain. All these recurrent images drive home the point that something has gone wrong with Lowry's universe in *Under the Volcano*.

They ram home the truth that the soul of Geoffrey's is sick. Soul is a recurrent word. The sickness in soul is owing to the thoroughly animistic world which surrounds Geoffrey. Animals, reptiles and birds play a major part in the field of symbolic references in the book. Geoffrey sits helplessly in the bathroom and watches a swarm of insects invading his consciousness: "A caterpillar started to wriggle toward him,

1. *Ibid*, p. 14.
2. *Ibid*., p. 14.
3. *Ibid*., p. 100.
4. *Ibid*., p. 73.

peering this way and that, with interrogatory antennae. A large cricket, with polished fuselage, clung to the curtain, swaying it slightly and cleaning its face like a cat, its eyes on stalks appearing to revolve in its head. He turned, expecting the caterpillar to be much nearer, but it too had turned, just slightly shifting its moorings. Now a scorpion was moving slowly across towards him. Suddenly the Consul rose, trembling in every limb. But it wasn't the scorpion he cared about. It was that, all at once, the thin shadows of isolated nails, the stains of murdered mosquitoes, the very scars and cracks of the wall, had begun to swarm, so that, wherever he looked, another insect was born, wriggling instantly toward his heart. It was as if, and this was what was most appalling, the whole insect world had somehow moved nearer and now was closing, rushing in upon him."[1]

It is not only the world of reptiles that fills him with sinister and uncanny feelings but animals too intrude into his mind during his stay at Senora Gregorio's Cantina El Bosque! "A starving pariah dog with the appearance of having lately been skinned had squeezed itself in after the last man; it looked up at the Consul with beady, gentle eyes. Then, thrusting down its poor wrecked dinghy of a chest from which raw withered breasts dropped it began to bow and scrape before him. Ah, the ingress of the animal kingdom! Earlier it had been the insects; now these were closing in upon him again, these animals...."[2]

The pariah dog or dogs which insistently attach themselves to Geoffrey may have a reference to the satanic black poodle which follows Goethe's Faust. This ingress of the animal kingdom into the human world has its insidious impact felt in the naming of some characters in the novel such as A Few Fleas, his father the Elephant (Roman Diasdado), the proprietor of the Farolito Cantina and the pimp is called stool pigeon.[3] All these characters have only the semblance of human anatomy but are bereft of essential human traits.

1. *Ibid.*, p. 148.
2. *Ibid.*, p. 228.
3. *Ibid*, p. 352.

Geoffrey is sick in the soul, because his whole consciousness has to contend with ferocious animals prowling and reptiles crawling in his mind. Through the preponderance of animal imagery the novelist evokes the consciousness of Geoffrey. The apocalyptic horse of death seen in the many moods and many settings during the twelve hours of the book's action is perhaps the most prominent animal imagery. It is Geoffrey who releases the restive horse at the Farolito that kills Yvonne in the stampede in the forest. In the First Chapter we find a horse with a rider in great excitement galloping at a breakneck speed.

Thus we find that imagery in *Under the Volcano* is expressive rather than imitative: "existing as a powerful, autonomous figure of speech from which radiate a host of evocative meanings."[1] These images have ever-expanding associations and it becomes difficult for a reader to restrict the varied meanings of the symbol. The Ferris wheel carries a multiplicity of interpretations, it is the wheel of Time, the wheel of the Law, the wheel of the Buddha. The image of the Volcano is a rich example. Sometimes it is Popocatepetl with ancient Mexican association that has stolen Geoffrey's heart away. He talks about the Mexican legend about Popocatepetl: "...in the tragic Indian legend Popocatepetl himself was strangely the dreamer: the fires of his warrior's love, never extinct in the poet's heart, burned eternally for Ixtaccihuatl, whom he had no sooner found than lost, and whom he guarded in her endless sleep...."[2]

It is Mount Etna with Tartarus at its base. It is Moby Dick, a great white whale, pursuing and becknoning Geoffrey. It is the Mountain of Delight for Geoffrey the pilgrim. It is the mighty mountain Himavat he believes he is ascending as he dies. All these several interpretations of a symbol cause reverberations in the mind of the reader and I agree with Heilman that in a Lowry novel, especially *Under the Volcano*, "the nexus are imaginative rather than casual, logical or

1. Smith, Anne: *The Art of Malcolm Lowry*, p. 131.
2. Lowry, Malcolm: *Under the Volcano*, p. 318.

chronological; hiatuses compel a high attention, dextrous leaps are called for. In such sense *Under the Volcano* may be understood as poetic—not in the sense that mystily atavistic syntax and a half-hearted Iambic hauteur as often in the seeking theatre, pass for poetic."[1]

The imaginative richness of the novel comes from the all-embracing mythic evocation, Joycean in character. The use of myth gives modern fiction a poetic character because myth is a favourite device with a modern poet like T.S. Eliot but the use of myth in *Under the Volcano* is different from that of in Joyce and Eliot. Stephen Spender makes a subtle distinction between the use of myth in Lowry's *Under the Volcano* and the creative works of Joyce and Eliot. In Lowry's novel the myth becomes an illustration of the fragmentary character of the phase of history of the thirties and the forties. In the First Chapter the writer says that Quauhnahuac splits at several places, when Christ is crucified. The crucifixion of Christ is not used here as a symbol of abounding love for the sinning humanity and a device for mastering the tormented psyche of Geoffrey. The myth of Christ is simply a picture of the disturbed period of the thirties and the forties through the character of Geoffrey and Geoffrey is a mask for the writer himself.

In Joyce and Eliot the fragmentary life in the present is related to the past and is evaluated in terms of the order of the past. The individual character is absorbed into cosmic consciousness transcending his personal self, as Tiresias in Eliot's *The Wast Land* is not an individual but the consciousness of the race. Stephen Spender's remark is highly illuminating: "They (Joyce and Eliot) use myths and symbols to get outside the times into the past of the tradition. Lowry uses them to exemplify "the times" to describe the Consul as illustration almost."[2]

There is substance, no doubt, in what Stephen Spender says but it is stretching things too far, when he observes that *Under the Volcano* lacks objectivity. The primal myth of Adam

1. The Sewanee Review, Vol. LV, 1947, p. 488.
2. Introduction to *Under the Volcano*, p. XII.

in the garden overgrown and seedy in Chapter Five in the novel is an attempt at enacting the fall from grace not of an individual Geoffrey but the story of the fall of Everyman from grace. The inscription on the wall of the house of M. Laruelle 'no pued, vivir sin amar' (we cannot live without loving) gives a truth that stands outside time and becomes a settled effect in the imagination of Geoffrey, though he fails to love Yvonne.

The technique of *Under the Volcano* is also cinematic. During his stay in Bonn in 1928 he became familiar with German Expressionist Theatre and film. The influence of cinema is noticeable in his choice of characters in *Under the Volcano*. M. Laruelle is a former French film producer and Yvonne is a movie actress of Hollywood. M. Laruelle contemplates a film script on Marlowe's Dr. Faustus. The impact of film is discernible in the 'kinetic writing'[1] of the novelist. Lowry creates "a moving landscape—or a still landscape against people moving"[2] ...and this style owes much to the cinema that is kinetic. We find a good specimen of this kinetic writing in Chapter One. "The rider of the horse was so drunk he was sprawling all over his mount, his stirrups lost, a feat in itself considering their size, and barely managing to hold on by the reins, though not once did he grasp the pommel to steady himself. The horse reared wildly, rebellious —half fearful, half contemptuous, perhaps, of its rider then it—catapulted in the direction of the car: the man, who seemed to be falling straight backwards at first, miraculously saved himself only to slip to one side like a trick rider, regained the saddle, slid, slipped, fell backwards—just saving himself each time, but always with the reins, never with the pommel, holding them in one hand now, the stirrups still unrecovered as he furiously beat the horse's flanks with the machete he had withdrawn from a long curved scabbard."[3]

The influence of film is noticeable in the use of the technique of flash-back. *Under the Volcano* begins with M. Laruelle's

1. *Ibid.*, p. XV.
2. *Ibid.*, p. XV.
3. Lowry, Malcolm: *Under the Volcano*, p. 22.

remembrance of the sequence of events leading to the ruin of Geoffrey. But it is not a mere retrospect of catastrophe that overtakes Geoffrey on the Day of the Dead November 1938. Laruelle's mind recedes still further to the boyhood scenes, when he finds himself in the company of Geoffrey as guests of the family of an English poet, Abraham Taskerson. It is flash-back within flash-back and abrupt shifts from extended scenes to close-ups.

The incorporation of Maquina Infernal in the novel is also symptomatic of cinematic art. Lowry saw Cocteau's Law Machine Infernale twice in Paris in May 1934. Cocteau's play is a variation of the Oedipus tragedy. A Fantome lets the audience know about the theme before the enactment of the play. At the conclusion of the preamble, the Fantome says: "Spectator, this machine you see here wound up to the full in such a way that the spring will slowly unwind the whole length of human life, is one of the most perfect constructed by the infernal Gods for the mathematical destruction of a human life."[1]

Lowry in his letter to the Cape reader treats *Under the Volcano* as a sort of machine and this conception of a novel as a machine owes to the film La Machine Infernale which has the precise working of a clock. Events unfold in a manner that bring about the ruin of Geoffrey. The spring of the machine has been unwinding the whole length of the Consul's life, bringing him inexorably to the morning of November 1938, the Day of the Dead.

The influence of cinema is also seen in the recurrent expression Las Manos de Orlac. It is on a poster advertising a film in which the chief actor is Peter Lorre. Just after her arrival Yvonne says to Hugh about Peter Lorre's film. "I think I've seen Peter Lorre movie somewhere. He's a great actor but it's a lousy picture...he thinks his hands are a murderer's or something and keeps washing the blood off them. Perhaps they are really a murderer's but I forget."[2]

1. Quoted in Douglas Day's *Malcolm Lowry: A Biography*, p. 323.
2. Lowry, Malcolm: *Under the Volcano*, p. 110.

Through the use of the poster of Peter Lorre's movie at several places in the novel the novelist tries to create the sense of evil and guilt proliferating.

Thus in *Under the Volcano* we find the presentment of the theme of Geoffrey, the British Consul, at Quauhnahuac with a compulsive longing for Yvonne mingled with the inability to love through the subtle technique of mythic evocation, recurrent motifs, interior monologues, flash-back and montage. When a novelist makes use of the twin devices of interior monologue and a tight allegorical pattern, he is prone to slide into two pitfalls. If he lays emphasis on a tightly bound allegory, the imaginative experience becomes attenuated and if he lays emphasis on imaginative experience, the novel becomes loose impressionism. Conrad Aiken, who is supposed to be the mentor of Lowry in the field of fiction, lacks the archet ectonic of his disciple and his interior monologue and recondite literary allusions in *Blue Voyage*, *Great Circle* and *King Coffin* are not unified into an artistic whole.

4

Lunar Caustic

What life have you if you have not life together?
There is no life that is not in community,
And no community not lived in praise of God

—T.S. Eliot Choruses from *The Rock*

(A) DOMINANT THEMES

Lunar Caustic is the result of Malcolm Lowry's first hand experience as a mental patient at Bellevue in New York. He reaches the city hospital of Bellevue after his separation from his wife Jan Gabrial. The fact of broken marriage exacerbated by alcoholism fills Lowry with agony and makes him commit himself to the psychiatric department of Bellevue hospital. He feels that the hospital will be a haven for the anguish gnawing at his soul. Though the novel has behind it the groundswell of Lowry's experiences as a patient suffering from traumatic experiences, it is much more than a literal transcription of what Lowry encounters at hospital.

This is because of the fact that Lowry lavishes a lot of care in composing his novels. He undertakes the story embodying his experiences at Bellevue hospital in 1934 but it takes twentyone long years to reach the finished version of *Lunar Caustic*. The story, incorporating his experiences as mental patient entitled *The Last Address*, undergoes modifications and appears in the form of a story *Swinging The Maelstrom* and these two stories the *The Last Address* and *Swinging The Maelstrom*, by Lowry's constant practice of assembling, annealing and revision 'splice' together and culminate in *Lunar Caustic*.

The interminable process of the sifting of materials and consequent organisation of experiences involved in *Lunar Caustic* supplies the much needed aesthetic distance. The novel grounded in the novelist's direct experience undergoes a transmutation and becomes an organised work of art. Thus motives that go into the making of *Lunar Caustic* have their genesis, no doubt, in intense private emotion of the novelist, but Lowry is such a brooding sort that he contemplates his private emotion and subjects it to such an artistic process, that the compulsive rhythm of the writer's private life attains the universality of the theme expected of a work of art. *Lunar Caustic* begins with Malcolm Lowry transposed in the character of the protagonist Bill Plantagenet, a seaman and a jazz musician, moving from one tavern to the other in the early morning in New York. His restless wanderings indicate or suggest that he must be looking for rather than trying to remember something. The disquiet that makes his search frantic is accentuated by the heat wave that has already taken a toll of more than a hundred New Yorkers.

In course of his brisk itinerary from saloon to saloon he appears to be some one who is perhaps led astray but a little reflection reveals that he is in the know of his destination. The saloons are only points on his circumference and his gaze is fixed on the hospital towering above the place he is roaming about. He has embarked on a mission. He tells us about his quest in explicit terms "I am sent to save my father, to find my son, to heal the eternal horror of three, to resolve the immedicable horror of opposites."[1]

The search thus has an existential character, It is something which relates to antinomies rooted in the very existence

1. Lowry, Malcolm: *Lunar Caustic*, p. 296.

of man—the antinomies of love and hate. The theme of unresolvable opposites, characterising human existence, mingles with the theme of the act of saving the father and finding the son.

The theme of the father becomes an obsession with Lowry, because from his very boyhood he does not have a rapport with the father in spite of the fact that he receives a lot of support from the father in terms of money. He receives the best what a son can receive from the father in the traditional manner of paternal solicitude but Lowry's mental make-up is such that he becomes a rebel and finds himself at logger-heads with the father. This search for the father expressed in the character of Bill Plantagenet, the protagonist of *Lunar Caustic*, is nothing but a projection of Lowry's estrangement from his father and his attempt at assuming father surrogate in Conrad Aiken and Melville.

This search for father is a search for one's identity, an attempt at a conscious articulation of the cultural heritage one belongs to. At one stroke Lowry snaps the bond of filial piety with his father Arthur O Lowry and declares his belief that he belongs to Conrad Aiken and Melville. The quest for finding the son is a search for someone who claims his love and affection but the tragedy with Malcolm Lowry is that he is incapable of love and this incapacity for love finds an expression in Bill Plantagenet's abandonment of his wife Ruth and his excessive indulgence in alcoholism. In short, the theme of ambivalent feelings such as love and hate, blended with the search for father and the son, stands out as Lowry's basic obsession.

The city hospital of Bellevue mirrors the predicament of Bill Plantagenet. It is a hideous place inhabited by neurotics, law-breakers and persons suffering from mortal diseases. All of them have come here in the hope of finding a cure for themselves. Bill Plantagenet is no better than the inmates of the city hospital, because he has broken off with his wife Ruth and has given himself up to boozing. He wants to shore up the ruin he has made of himself by his descent into the abyss of mire and squalor. At one place in the novel he makes self-introspection and wants to know why he has come to this doleful place. He believes that "...he had voyaged downward to the foul core of his world; here was the true meaning underneath all the loud inflamed words, the squealing headlines, the arrogant years".[1]

If the city hospital is the sordid part of his world, it also has a silver lining in its all-pervasive gloom. Looking at the doctor he feels that he is perhaps "...the cure, the wisdom, and vision, the more patient still...And goodness was here too—he glanced at his two friends—Yes, by what miracle did it come about that compassion and love were here too?..."[2]

Though Bill Plantagenet finds in the figure of Dr. Claggart, an emblem of something that pierces the pall of gloom that has descended on the city hospital, there is no denying the fact that, Dr. Claggart alongwith the inmates of the hospital, stands for uncomplaining acceptance of degeneration. Bill Plantagenet has the brutal frankness of saying to Dr. Claggart in his face that "...you're as resigned as your wretched patients,..."[3]

The acquiescence of Dr. Claggart is seen in the light of the nerve-wracking woık he does for a paltry remuneration. Plantagenet wonders at the supine resignation of the doctor who is under-paid and shockingly over-worked. Through the character of Plantagenet the novelist brings to light the theme of people of our times, who are so foul and debased, that they go on reconciling themselves to any indignity that is heaped on them. Plantagenet's conversation with the doctor is illustrative of the rot that festers in humanity: "But good Christ, Doctor, in this place the people, the patients, are resigned, resigned! Can't you see the horror, the horror of men's uncomplaining acceptance of his own degeneration ?"[4] To Plantagenet Dr. Claggart, instead of making an attempt at stemming the tide of abject surrender of humanity in

1. Lowry, Malcolm: *Lunar Caustic*, p. 316.
2. *Ibid.*
3. *Ibid.*, pp. 327-28.
4. *Ibid.*, p. 328.

the face of degeneration, perpetuates it through the city hospital of Bellevue. Bill Plantagenet, who, too, has given way to forces of the degeneration, feels the necessity of something which, instead of adjusting people to the system in the manner of Dr. Claggart, finds a mode of resurrection.

Thus, two contrasted themes—the theme of acceptance of the rot without any demur and the urge for new life cleansed of the soot and grime of those who are fallen into the pit—are woven into the explicit statement of the idea of saving the father and finding the son and discovering the horror of opposites. It is the urge for a new life pulsating with exuberance which will contain the onrush of apathy, stupor and objection, threatening to devour humanity.

It is to the credit of Bill Plantagenet that in spite of his being a victim of base passions, he blasts Dr. Claggart's pretension to find a cure for his patients.... "Many who are supposed to be mad here, as opposed to the ones who are drunks, are simply people who perhaps once saw, however confusedly, the necessity for change in themselves, for rebirth, that's the word".[1] Bill Plantagenet in support of his contention, cites the case of Battle.

Battle has boundless energy but because of the technique of Dr. Claggart to persistently try and adjust patients to the system, all the magnificent power goes to waste: of course now he wont't hurt a fly, he has grown to like degeneration. But Dr. Claggart takes a different view of the inmates of the hospital. His approach is pragmatic and down-to-earth. He has no illusions about life and he wants to make the best of unbeglamoured world. Thus the pragmatism of Dr. Claggart wrestles with the momentary visions Bill Plantagenet sees.

To Bill Plantagenet, Garry who cuts the throat of a child with a broken bottle, is sensitive and has a visionary strain. But the wooden and mechanical treatment of Dr. Claggart kills his visionary gleam and makes a ruin of his life by keeping him within the confines of hospital. The two different strains of

1. Lowry, Malcolm: *Lunar Caustic*, p. 328.

pragmatism and visionary gleam collide in the novel. To Claggart, Garry stands for fantasy but to Bill Plantagenet, Garry is no ordinary fabricator of tell-tales. Garry is the embodiment of the perennial urge in man to create both order and chaos.

By blasting away the foul and murky in life he wants to create something that throbs with life. But Claggart is no visionary and he is a representative of the idea of life that appeals to common sense. The puppet-show arranged under his supervision at hospital has the purpose of exerting a cool and a sober influence on lunatics. The show is designed for the socialisation of lunatics who most of the time lie curled up in their inner Africa. The brooding and sulking spirit of the individual is kept in abeyance for a while, so that he may forget the grief in communal experience. It is the theme of the isolation and ennui of the individual, pitted against community, which brings people out of the cramped shell of their wounded individuality. The puppet-show is also designed for controlling emotional outbursts of the hospital.

But the theme of pragmatism, socialisation and restraint in the individual, presented through Dr. Claggart and his puppet-show, comes into conflict with the life of dreams and visions espoused by Bill Plantagenet. It is the life of dreams and vision that finds a beautiful evocation in Section X of the novella. The scene in which Bill Plantagenet outside Claggart's office watches the park, when thunder rumbles and a deluge is imminent, is a turning-point in the thematic organisation of the novella.

The rich sensuous details—recreating the rainbow-like effect of the children's fountain, lovers running for shelter, laughing, their arms around one another and the riven trees yearning into the gloom lit by the heliotrope of the lightning are suggestive of the fact that even in his hour of degeneration some redeeming features are left in Bill Plantagenet. Through Bill Plantagenet's observation of life in the park in Section X of the novella, Lowry presents, though fitfully, the ineffable grace of life that wrestles with all-pervasive gloom.

The theme of ineffable grace, that withstands the onslaughts of vile passions, is seen in Bill Plantagenet's gesture of fellow-feeling and comradeship, when he buys some stamps for Garry and oranges worth a dollar for Kalowsky. The brooding and sulking self of Bill Plantagenet emerges from his inner Africa and enters into a loving relationship with Garry and Kalowsky but the theme of comradeship is not sustained, because the novelist as well as the protagonist Bill Plantagenet becomes despondent and gives way to sloth and stupor.

It is only in Section XI of the novella that Bill Plantagenet makes the heroic battle of expunging vile passions and launching a new life. In this mood of sublime resolution for carving a new life he suddenly becomes enraged and hurls the bottle against the obscene sketch of a girl, believing that by doing so, he will wipe out indecency, cruelty, hideousness and injustice in the world.

Bill Plantagenet, who at the outset of the novel finds himself pursued by demons in his inner Africa, makes a resolve to come out of the sinister shell of his sordid preoccupations with a view to embarking on a life of health and sanity. This impulse to health and sanity in Bill Plantagenet is antithetical to the impulse to self-extinction characteristic of Geoffrey Firmin in Lowry's *Under the Volcano.* This is because *Lunar Caustic* is designed differently from *Under the Valcano.* Talking about his scheme in *Under the Volcano* and *Lunar Caustic,* Malcolm Lowry, in his letter to Albert Erskin, observes: "*Under the Volcano* was originally planned as the inferno part of a Dantesque trilogy to be called *The Voyage That Never Ends. Lunar Caustic* was the purgatorial part...".[1]

George Firmain of *Under the Volcano* knows that the tragedy of his life arises from his incapacity for love. He wants to save himself from ruin and fitfully makes attempts at redeeming himself by the act of love but it all remains a pious resolution and he sinks into his inner Africa of desolation. But Bill Plantagenet overtly in Section XI and in a subterranean way in sections other than Section XI works for

1. Lowry, Malcolm: Selected Letters, (Capricorn Books, New York, 1969), p. 113.

his salvation by feeding the flame of love with the faggot of his own awareness of the imperatives of love.

It is this urge for a life of love and sanity which makes him question the very efficacy of Dr. Claggart's method of treating souls that are sick. A remedy may be found for physical ailments but ailments. that have their roots in either the mind or the soul of a man require a different treatment for the malaise. The patient suffering from sickness in mind or soul is to be handled with great delicacy and imagination. The pragmatist in Dr. Claggart is not in a position to comprehend the malady afflicting a myth-maker like Garry. Unless an imaginative rapport is established with the patient, the patient has no chance of recovery. Dr. Claggart shows a lack of understanding of his patients on the imaginative plane in spite of all his goodness and solicitude for his patients.

The Consul of *Under the Volcano* is a character of great powers but all the intellectual prowess of the Consul is of no avail to him, because he sadly lacks the mighty principle of love. All the time he is seen ruminating on finding the cause for the failure of his life. Sometimes he shows remarkable clairvoyance by grasping the cause of his undoing but when the question of informing his life with the mighty principle of love comes, he cuts a very sorry figure. He makes a wreck of himself. because love and sympathy depart from his life in the crucial hour, though he makes a loud protestation all the time that the absence of love is nothing but a denial of life.

In *Lunar Caustic* the protagonist, Bill Plantagenet, is concerned with the theme of transcending the limited self sunk in low passions for a perception of a life suffused with love and sympathy. Its manifestation is noticeable in Bill Plantagenet buying oranges for Garry and Kalowsky. The gift of oranges is a magnanimous gesture on the part of a patient at a mental hospital who shows a perception much more remarkable than the perception of the practising psychiatrist that the cure of the patient lies in love and not in making a mechanical adjustment to the system.

The cure lies in the imaginative leap, an insight into what lies at the root of the malady. Without the vision of a Rimbaud the malady lies concealed and the patient shut up in the cark recess of his heart. The imaginative leap is possible, when a person makes a burial of the past and prepares himself for a life of noble passions. To Claggart, the frail but unceasing myth-making power is a trash when he says... "These stories take the form of illiterate fables, or children's stories."[1] But to Bill Plantagenet, Garry is a sensitive child and he is being killed in the suffocating atmosphere of Bellevue.

Garry, whose stories are about things collapsing, falling apart and things buried in all the wreckage, is also the teller of tales of a life radiant and exuberant. Thus if Lowry, through the character of Bill Plantagenet, talks about a world macabre and nightmarish, very much akin to Dana Hilliot of *Ultramarine*, suffering the experience of complete self-annihilation, he combines this murky and sinister world of his heroes in his earlier two novels (*Ultramarine* and *Under the Volcano*) with an experience all aglow with the prospect of a journey into the bourne of enchantment in *Lunar Caustic*.

In Section X Bill Plantagenet is possessed by a delicious sense of freedom, a sense of being already outside, free to run with the wind if he wished, free to run as far away from the hospital as he liked. This sense of a life charged with abounding exhilaration is a triumph over the harrowing experience of Bill Plantagenet in New York which he considers to be a city of dreadful night. In Section X Bill Plantagenet sees the vision of New York crystallised therefore an instant, glittering, illuminated by a celestial brilliance.

Though this picture of celestial brilliance is shown to be reclaimed by dark, by the pandemonium of avalanche of falling coal, mingling in his brain with a picture of the mechanic calamity of rocking city, with the screaming of suicides, of girls tortured in hotels for transients, of people burning to death in vice dens, there is no gainsaying the fact that Lowry's theme of damnation and salvation go hand in hand from the start to the finish of his career in varying proportions. If *Under the Volcano* is a journey through inferno, *Lunar Caustic* is marked by a strong desire for getting

1. Lowry, Malcolm: *Lunar Caustic*, p. 331.

away from the life of appalling isolation into a life of freedom.

In short, one of the themes, constituting *Lunar Caustic*, is the horror of our civilization impining on the mind of a highly sensitive temperament such as Bill Plantagenet. The city of New York encompasses the horrors of the civilization which is out of joint and Bill Plantagenet, a jazz musician, who is moving from place to place, exposes himself to the horrors of the city. It is quite strange that Bill Plantagenet is not benumbed by the terrors of life. He retains his values and upholds them in the face of the tide of vulgarity swamping everything. Apparently Bill Plantagenet is a character without an identity, because sometimes he says that he is a jazz musician and sometimes he assumes the name of S.S. Lawhill which is nothing but the name of a ship. The identity of Bill Plantagenet becomes confounded but Bill Plantagenet is not gutless. He has the toughness of spirit which knows how to withstand the sinister forces sapping a man's hold on life. The reference to Melville in the novel is nothing but underpinning the novel with unbreakable stuff Melville is made of.

Garry neither belongs to the category of poor lunatics nor of subtle lunatics on account of the irrepressible myth-making power in him. All sedulous attempts of Dr. Claggart at restoring sanity to Garry go awry in the face of the perennial impulse in Garry to make up stories in spite of countless impediments undermining his hold on life. It is this fact of Garry as an arch fabulist that makes him stand out unique in the midst of patients at Bellevue who bow down to earth with their neuroses. The pall of gloom arising from neurosis also touches Garry but Garry has something unique about his character that saves him from being a mere flotsam tossed to and fro by unremitting despair.

Some readers may dismiss Garry as a character obsessed with the stories of dissolution and annihilation but Garry is much more than a prophet of cynicism. Those who believe that Garry is a cynic cite the passage about the barge loaded with coal which sinks when the rope snaps. To Garry the large barge smashed and broken symbolises tragedy lurking in life. This perception of tragedy dogging at a man's life is a half-truth. The whole truth comes to a man, when he joins it to a man's inherent power to take things in his stride. It is the philosophy of 'Grieve not' which sustains a man through all vicissitudes. This philosophy of exaltation in the face of all odds is evident in Garry recounting the tale of a sea-man. He speaks of a boat sailing on the bosom of the main when the storm is on the deep and the angry sea roars. All feel shattered in a cabin and none dares stir out. All are gripped with the fear of utter ruin but the straggle is on and the boat is anchored safe in the harbour next day. The story relating to the killing of the whale, salting it and packing it in the barrels is the tale of adventure. This tale of adventure is the story of a man who relishes wrestling with set-backs that come his way. Thus, if Garry weaves tales of utter wreck and ruin, he also tells us stories about life throbbing with vigour and this invincible urge in Garry stands in a sharp contrast to the third member of the triad Kalowsky. Kalowsky is melancholy and disconsolate all through the novel. He appears to be a character completely drained of the zest for life. He suffers from exhaustion and when he finds Garry recounting tales of destruction, he recoils and requests Garry to relate stories that act as a soothing balm to his afflicted nerves. Hs can't stomach Garry talking about the barge sinking to the bottom of the sea and the story of Pomeii crumbling and falling to the ground. He is in dire need of a palliative, he seeks a lotion for his soul writhing with anguish. He, therefore, says to Garry all the time that he should tell him 'humouristic stories'.

To Kalowsky, the wandering Jew, humouristic stories mean stories that are about the pleasant facts of life. Kalowsky is fed up with life and has perhaps lost the battle of life. He is a spent swimmer who wants to clutch at a drifting straw for his survival.

(B) ART OF CHARACTERIZATION

Lunar Caustic is a symbolist fable depicting the horrors of our civilization epitomised by the city of New York, especially

Bellevue hospital, through its protagonist Bill Plantagenet. Symbolist fables as such are considered to be deficient in exuberance of life, because the maker of a fable is all the time intent on subordinating the profusion of details of individual lives to the overall controlling design of the fable. But it is to the credit of Malcolm Lowry, that in spite of the tight scheme of his fable, he sees to it that the contours of his individual characters are preserved.

The theme of *Lunar Caustic* is refracted, no doubt, through the consciousness of Bill Plantagenet but other characters such as Kalowsky, Garry, Battle and Dr. Claggart are not merely subsidiary to Bill Plantagenet. All these secondary characters other than Bill Plantagenet with their life-patterns come to the reader as images of life interacting with Bill Plantagenet and weave the rich fable of *Lunar Caustic*. It also shows how Malcolm Lowry successfully grapples with the problem of the creation of individual character vis-a-vis the overall design of the novella. Individual characters mesh well with the form of the fable.

Apart from the five main human characters such as Bill Plantagenet, Kalowsky, Garry, Battle and Dr. Claggart the novella has a puppeteer with his troupe comprising Caspar-Punch, Judy and the chief of the African tribe. The puppet-show is not only composed of human characters but has also some sinister demonic agents controlling the course of the puppet-show. The world of the puppeteer imparts a Kafka-like dimension of nightmarish experience which makes a shiver run down the spine of the reader. The characterization of the novella moves not only in the realm of men but also in the chimera-like world of giants guiding the course of the puppet-show.

Characters in the novella fall into three groups. The first group is composed of characters such as Bill Plantagenet, Kalowsky and Garry. They have a great affinity, they are spiritually akin to one another. The triad made up of Bill Plantagenet, Kalowsky and Garry is not on emotional wave-length with Dr. Claggart.

Bill Plantagenet who is the hero of the novella is an Englishman voluntarily sojourning at Bellevue hospital in New York intended for mental patients. The second is Kalowsky who is a Lithuanian Jew who is also an inmate along with Bill Plantagenet of the Observation Ward of Bellevue hospital. The third is a thirteen-year-old boy named Garry receiving treatment in the company of Bill Plantagenet and Kalowsky after he has cut the throat of a girl with a broken bottle. Garry who is charged with insanity hopes to recover mental health at Bellevue.

This triad of Bill Plantagenet, Kalowsky and Garry stands in a sharp contrast to Dr. Claggart. Dr. Claggart is the treating surgeon at Bellevue hospital where Bill Plantagenet, Kalowsky and Garry are supposed to retrieve health and sanity. The contrast between the treating surgeon and his patients is a source of tension in the novella. There is no denying the fact that patients hope to get solace to their afflicted nerves under the maternal care of the doctor but the three patients, just referred to, do not get along with the doctor. They are at logger-heads with him. Dr. Claggart forms the second category along with the hornifaced nurse and the puppeteer.

The third category is made up of Battle, a Negro fireman, who has knocked out the teeth of an engineer on the deck of the ship. Battle has a string of couplets acting as a foil to the Rimbaud-like muth-making power of Garry.

A casual reader who has not attuned himself to the richer timbre of the novella will take it as an account of a neurotic Bill Plantagenet for whom the stars of the firmament were 'wounds opening in his being'[1], multiple duplications of agony to remedy him. He may take it as a tale of degeneration, but Lowry through the limited diversity of characters makes a complex world, though he says that the protagonist Bill Plantagenet has an affinity with the simplistic vision of Garry.

1. Lowry, Malcolm: *Lunar Caustic*, p. 304.

Though Bill Plantagenet has some striking parallel with the novelist, he is not a mere replica of the writer. It speaks well for Lowry that he takes pains to give an independent identity to Bill Plantagenet. The point of similarity between Lowry and his principal character Bill Plantagenet in *Lunar Caustic* relates to their alcoholism and their indifference and non-chalance in their relations with their wives. The fact of alcoholism and indifference to wives is central to Lowry and his chief character Bill Plantagenet in *Lunar Caustic*, because those two cardinal facts of their love prove to be the cause of their undoing. It is not known whether love of alcohol makes Lowry and his alter-ego Bill Plantagenet fail their wives Jan and Ruth respectively or whether their incapacity for enduring love for their wives makes them addicts of wine.

But *Lunar Caustic*, which in the words of Lowry is a master-work, is not a mere tale of alcoholism.[1] In course of his rambling conversation with Dr. Claggart, Bill Plantagenet emphatically declares, "Drinking is not my problem." The trouble lies deeper inside his psyche and all through the novella Bill Plantagenet, who is supposed to be Lowry's second-self, wrestles with the epistemological side of the problem which not only fills Bill Plantagenet with unrest but has become the bane of the entire civilization. Richard K. Cross, in *Malcolm Lowry: A Preface to his Fiction*, rightly observes that Lowry through Bill Plantagenet challenges the "opacity of the world"[2] with the potent weapon of the imagination.

The problem that bedevils Bill Plantagenet is the problem of present day humanity cut off from sanctions, moral and metaphysical. The awful isolation from the moral and metaphysical universe has engendered utter confusion which in the words of Garry, encompasses not only the individual but the whole of the world. Bill Plantagenet himself in his nightmarish soliloquy says,... "that even Nature herself is shot through with jitteriness."[3] In this chaotic state of affairs, when

1. Lowry, Malcolm: *Selected Letters*, p. 292.
2. Cross K. Richard: *Malcolm Lowry*, p. 19.
3. Lowry, Malcolm: *Lunar Caustic*, p. 308.

everything is in a shambles, Bill Plantagenet is to be taken to be a character apart from his creator Malcolm Lowry waging a war with his problems.

In *Lunar Caustic* he imagines himself abandoned... "on his final frontier".[1] The 'final frontier' is a chilling expression which succinctly evokes the solitary state of an individual fighting for his soul on his own. The lone fighter striving hard for his salvation is riddled with the sense of shame and guilt. He is battered and mutilated and has nothing to lean on and as a result of this he wages a terrible battle.

The tool coming to his rescue is the never-failing desire for expiation of crimes committed. Bill Plantagenet has metaphorically been named Mr. Remorse. Thus *Lunar Caustic*, which is supposed to be the story of a man unable to disentangle himself from the vice of drinking, becomes the story of a man given to penitence. It thus moves away from alcoholism with which Lowry is obsessed and becomes an account of how poignantly Bill Plantagenet strives for peeling off the layers of vices for a luminous self. In short, Lowry, in *Lunar Caustic*, instead of writing a sordid tale of his alcoholism, contemplates the problem of how life can be terrifying, when it is at a remove from the life-giving forces of love and compassion.

The novelist develops this theme through the deft touches of character-creation. The character of Bill Plantagenet reveals more through a gradual recalling of the past. He feelingly rakes up the past, picks up telling details, pieces them together and presents the fragments of his life with the semblance of coherence to Dr. Claggart under whose care he convalesces at Bellevue Hospital in New York. When Dr. Claggart wants to know from Bill Plantagenet the cause of his failure as a azz musician, he, in a bland manner, holds the smallness of his hands responsible for his failure: "I've been playing in dives. But it's my hands, my hands, look 'he held them out, shaking.' They're not big enough for a real pianist, I can't stretch over an octave on a piano. On a guitar I fake all the time".[2]

1. *Ibid.*, p. 317.

2. Lowry, Malcolm: *Lunar Caustic*, p. 302.

The doctor has such a keen perception that he instantaneouly finds out what is wrong with him. It is Bill Plantagenet's gesture of putting his head down, burying it under the pillow and his looking at the doctor furtively mingled with a certain rebelliousness, gives Dr. Claggart a handle for probing the malaise lurking inside Bill Plantagenet. Dr. Claggart pierces the veil of the specious plea of Bill Plantagenet by reaching the core of the truth: "Perhaps it was your heart you couldn't make stretch an octave".[1]

This comment of Dr. Claggart disarms Bill Plantagenet and makes him quite vulnerable. It is as if Dr. Claggart has discovered the Achilles' heel of Bill Plantagenet and made him defenceless. Bill Plantagenet, who puts on a veneer with a view to obscuring the truth, finds a big rent in his armour and makes a hideous disclosure about his wife Ruth: 'I don't know. I don't care. Hell with her! she only brought me back as a sort of souvenir from Europe.'[2] The vehemence of his utterance shows that Bill Plantagenet has completely broken off with Ruth but his later ruminations tell a different story.

In those broodings over the past he comes to us not as a character who has turned his back on Ruth but appears to be a character bruised and lacerated with the sense of unfulfilled love. Pleasant r emories of Ruth swarm into his consciousness! "How delighted Ruth had been that day long ago because they had a cabin on top deck of the Providence! It was his first day in New York, summer then too, and they had paced the deck arm-in-arm. In the evening they had wandered around the ancient, lacquered ship, like a vast London hotel with its gilt stairways."[3]

This loving promenade of Bill Plantagenet on the deck of the cabin is one side of the coin, radiant with amour and this mood of dalliance has to be seen along with the mood of disdainful rejection of Ruth. Bill Plantagenet is no Tennysonian

1. Lowry, Malcolm: *Lunar Caustic*, p. 303.
2. *Ibid.*, pp. 302-303.
3. *Ibid.*, p. 340.

Lotus-eater browsing through the land of sweet sensations. He is a character of our times, who nurses no illusions about life and looks at reality, as it is in itself.

Lowry who is taken to be a writer in the romantic mode does not luxuriate in gaiety. He has the clairvoyance to see both beauty and ugliness: "What had they not learned about the world and each other in that cabin so high up in the ship? They had not learned that with all the beauty of the evening, the softness of the night, the tenderness of the blue morning, that every beat of the engine which took them nearer to New Bedford, nearer to Herman Melville, was also taking them nearer to their own white whale, their own destruction."[1]

From this paragraph it is abundantly clear that Lowry's intention behind the creation of Bill Plantagenet is quite serious. Plantagenet's problem is not, as he boldly avers, that of the depravity of an alcoholic wreck. Putting off all blinkers from his eyes, Plantagenet is face-to-face with the gritty reality of unbeglamoured world of ours but his perception of the vileness of the world is not that of a cynic or a misanthrope, heaping venom and indignity on man. From the outside Plantagenet comes to us as a character without moral imagination, a character sunk in the abyss of low passions and doing dirt on the hallowed values of life. But on a little reflection we find that he is very much alive to moral values.

He is so much supped with the horror of life in the vein of Conrad's Mistah Kurtz in *The Heart of Darkness*, that his very exclamation 'Horror' becomes a positive moral affirmation. In his talk with Dr. Claggart, Bill Plantagenet poses the problem of a sharp moral appraisal of life: But my God, it's horror—and it's all there waiting for me: the ghosts on the window blind, the scarlet snowshoe, the whispering of lost opportunities, and all the fury, the anguish, the remorse, the voices, voices, voices, voices; the doll that turns to Ruth, the brownstone-brimstone—fronts transformed into judges..."[2]

The mature moral imagination Bill Plantagenet exhibits recalls to nd the moral imagination of French Symbolists

1. *Ibid.*, p. 341.
2. *Ibid.*, p. 334.

such as Baudelaire and Rimbaud who, through the artistic presentment of the images of filth and squalor, give their moral universe. However, the imagination of Lowry is less moral and more religious. This religious imagination of Lowry has come to him through his saturation with evil and the statement of Blake he cites in the novella "The road of excess leads to the Palace of Wisdom".[1]

It may be argued that wisdom is fitful and momentary in the novella. But the striving for grace is ceaseless not only in the novella but all through Lowry's works. It is quite difficult to agree with Richard K. Cross that 'a thwarted religious sensibility'[2] characterises the protagonists of both *Lunar Caustic* and *Under the Volcano*.

I find fault with Richard K. Cross who observes that the protagonists of *Lunar Caustic* and *Under the Volcano* have a thwarted religious sensibility. It is not expected of all writers to be religious conformists in the vein of a George Herbert or a Coventry Patmore subscribing to the serenity of faith in their Christian Gods.

The expression of a sustained religious faith in a God of one's choice is not the hallmark of the Lowry universe. In the vein of Donne, Lowry is engaged in a constant warfare within his psyche. He falls into the blood and mire of the world but he also shows the readiness of mind to come out of the slough of gloom and despondency. Richard K. Cross's appraisal of Lowry is correct, when he says that the protagonists of *Lunar Caustic* and *Under the Volcano* yearn for a grace that will deliver them from the hell of self-involvement. It is the "louse of conscience"[3] that keeps Bill Plantagenet always on his toes, drawing up his strategies for putting down the rebellious forces in his mind, when he finds himself on the final frontier of life.

This state of preparedness in Bill Plantagenet to meet with adversaries in the mind rightly gives Lowry the sanction for calling *Lunar Caustic* the purgatorio part of his contemplated

1. *Ibid.*
2. Cross K. Richard: *Malcolm Lowry: A Preface to His Fiction*, p. 23.
3. Lowry, Malcolm: *Lunar Caustic*, p. 308.

trilogy of *The Voyage that Never Ends*. Richard K. Cross's observation: "For all the talk of rebirth, the suffering Lowry depicts in the novella remains that of the damned rather than those in the process of being redeemed"[1] is a bit wide of the mark.

It is the surge of remorse in Bill Plantagenet which has the effect of cleansing him of all nightmarish experiences and consequently prepares him for the heroic pursuit in the concluding section of the novella. Bill Plantagenet experiences the stirring of a life instinct with a noble destiny, when he flings a bottle to smash into bits the obscene sketch of a girl chalked on the wall. He feels ennobled by striking the provocative portrait of a girl and registers his opposition to "... indecency, the cruelty, the hideousness, the filth and injustice in the world".[2] To say that the purgatorial fire does not burn in the novella is to ignore the searching question Bill Plantagenet poses to Dr. Claggart, knocking the bottom out of his profession of psychiatry: "But good Christ Doctor, in this place the people, the patients, are resigned, resigned! Can't you see "the horror, the horror of men's uncomplaining acceptance of his own degeneration"?[3] The doctor is doing a patch work, he is a surgeon who himself is smashed but undertakes the job of sending soldiers who are battered and whose nerves have gone to pieces. It is an irony that a man like Dr. Claggart, who is himself battered, thinks of making soldiers, spent and exhausted, brace up for another battle.

Bill Plantagenet does not have a faith in a world of make-believe; he wants to blast away the outworn in order to create a new life and with candour he speaks of the glimmer of rebirth even in patients who are sunk in stupor at Bellevue 'Because many who are supposed to be mad here, as opposed to the ones who are drunks, are simply people who perhaps once saw, however confusedly, the necessity for change in themselves, for rebirth, that's the word'.[4]

1. Cross K. Richard: *Malcolm Lowry*, p. 24.
2. Lowry, Malcolm: *Lunar Caustic*, p. 346.
3. *Ibid* , p. 328.
4. *Ibid.*, p. 328.

Bill Plantagenet who is the leading light of the triad steals the show but the other two members of the triad, namely Garry and Kalowsky, have their individual lives. Garry, a thirteen-year-old American boy, who is an inmate of Bellevue City hospital with the accusation on his head that he has cut the throat of a girl with a broken bottle, is crazy, no doubt, but endears himself to all. The secret of his popularity lies in the agility of his mind in making up stories: . . . "Wherever I am if I'm up in the air, or under the sea, or in the mountains, anywhere—I can tell a story. No matter where you put me even in prison. I can be sitting, not sitting. Eating, not eating. I can put the whole thing into that story, that's what makes it a story."[1] This creative impluse redeems Garry and makes readers sit up and give a second thought to Lowry's creation of Garry.

To Kalowsky, Garry a member of the triad, comes as a portrait of Rimbaud. This allusion to Rimbaud is not an attempt at making the novella ponderous and heavy by thrusting greatness on a crazy character such as Garry. The parallel between Garry and Rimbaud is rooted in their concern for things that are murky and sordid. Stories Garry weave are about disaster smeared over the universe and thus stories that are about the dark night of the soul have a likeness to Rimbaud who writes in 1871: "Now, I am degrading myself as much as possible. Why? I want to be a poet and am working hard for to make myself a seer. . . it is a question of reaching the unknown by the derangement of all the senses."[2]

The fact that Garry is crazy and has cut the throat of a girl with a broken bottle is nothing but the derangement of senses of which Rimbaud speaks. This deliberate distortion of the mind is insanity but it is not insanity, if it is seen in the perspective the novella builds. In this context it is rewarding, if we take into account the subtle distinction between poor lunatics "and subtle lunatics"[3] in the novella. In a world where neurotic behaviour is the rule, more 'subtle lunatics'

1. *Ibid.*, p. 300.
2. Quoted by Douglas Day in *Malcolm Lowry: A Biography*, p. 202.
3. Lowry, Malcolm: *Lunar Caustic*, p. 317.

exert almost supreme hegemony by adjusting 'poor lunatics' to mischievous world.

(C) TECHNIQUE

The question of technique in Malcolm Lowry's *Lunar Caustic* involves a discussion of Expressionism with which he has great kinship. Expressionism, in which Malcolm Lowry is much soaked, is a movement in the first quarter of the twentieth century against realism and naturalism. Realists and naturalists keep close to the facts of the objective world but Expressionists, instead of reproducing the objective reality of the world, present the subjective reality of feelings which objects and events arouse. In a letter to Jonathan Cape, Malcolm Lowry speaks of his "rebellion"[1] against the realist school with its photographic fidelity in adhering to the externals of life. He is after "a new form, a new approach to reality itself",[2] he avers, in a letter to Albert Erskine and the perspective on reality he develops is that of an Expressionist who undermines the foundations of realistic art and renders visible "soul-states and the violent emotions welling up from the innermost recesses of the subconscious..."[3].

The anti-mimetic approach typical of an Expressionist is seen at its best in Malcolm Lowry's presentment of the soul of Bill Plantagenet, the protagonist of *Lunar Caustic,* writhing in anguish. Unlike realists, Malcolm Lowry strives to break down the frontier between subjective and objective reality and to superimpose the subjective reality of Bill Plantagenet upon the external world. In section X of *Lunar Caustic* this blurring of boundaries between subjective and objective reality is seen in its most menacing form. Bill Plantagenet is shaken by despair resulting from the overwhelming sense of guilt tearing away his vitals and in this mood of dejection the surrounding landscape becomes an extension of his languishing self losing all its autonomy.

1. Lowry, Malcolm: *Selected Letters*, p. 68.
2. *Ibid.*, p. 330.
3. Quoted by Anne Smith in *The Art of Malcolm Lowry*, p. 96.

The colossal despair is all-pervasive and casts the pall of sinister blackness over the East River: "All at once, watching the strange traffic upon it, he fancied that the East River was as delirious, as haunted as the mind that brooded over it, it was a mad river of grotesque mastless steamers, of flat barges slipping along silent as water snakes, a river of railroad boats the shape of army tanks with their askew funnels appearing to have been built on to outriggers, they were stranger half ships, preposterously high out of the water with naked propellers thrashing like tuna fish, with single masts out of alignment. This world of the river was one where everything was uncompleted while functioning in degeneration, from which as from Garry's barge, the image of their own shattered or unformed souls was cast back at them."[1]

The deliberate disruption of spatial continuity, that makes Malcolm Lowry change 'good honest ships'[2] into 'nightmare ships' on the East River, is a typical Expressionist stylistic device. The grotesque distortion Malcolm Lowry takes recourse to is an Expressionist stylistic element making vivid the derangement wrought in Bill Plantagenets' psyche by guilt and remorse by fastening it on the outer landscape. In the effort to superimpose agony raging in the soul of the protagonist of *Lunar Caustic* upon the objective world things, inner and outer, real and fantastic, become confused and interchanged. In this attempt at grafting inner confusion upon objective reality, landscapes appear to have assumed a sinister and menacing form. They become highly revealing and make palpable and vivid emotional states.

In *Lunar Caustic* Bill Plantagenets' agony which was like a great lidless eye finds its symbolic diagram in the landscape: "Darkness was falling; through the clearing haze the stars came out, Over the broken horizon the Scorpion was crawling. There was the red, dying sun, Antares. To the South-east, the Retreat of the Howling Dog appeared. The Stars taking their places were wounds opening in his being, multiple duplications of that agony, of that eye. The constellations might have

1. Lowry, Malcolm: *Lunar Caustic*, pp. 338-39.
2. *Ibid.*, p. 338.

been monstrosities in the delirium of God. Disaster seemed smeared over the whole universe. It was as if he were living in the pre-existence of some unimaginable catastrophe and he steadied himself against the sill, feeling the doomed earth itself stagger in its heaving spastic flight towards the Hercules Butterfly."[1] The landscape not only mirrors the inner confusion in Bill Plantagenet but also participates in his destruction, as it does in *Under the Volcano*.

This Expressionist technique of Malcolm Lowry, which seeks to do away with the boundary between subjective and objective reality and to superimpose the subjective reality upon the external world, is susceptible to the charge of being nothing but a receptacle seizing moment to moment sensations swarming the consciousness of the protagonist. A novelist, with an Expressionist vision such as Malcolm Lowry, concerned with the picturing of violent emotions welling up from the subconscious, is supposed to write a morbid tale, a phantasmagoria, a macabre dance of sinister forces impairing the very being of man. Malcolm Lowry is a conscientious craftsman and he is aware of the pitfall inherent in the Expressionist predilection for self-portraiture.

Of great consideration to him is the portrayal of individual soul-states, the soul-states of characters such as Bill Plantagenet in *Lunar Caustic* but of equal importance is the universal soul. His novels are built out of the dialectics of intense subjectivism wrestling with values of a cosmic nature. Bill Plantagenet's predicament is peculiar to him, no doubt, but like Geoffrey Firmin in *Under the Volcano* he embodies the soul of modern Western man on the edge of a precipice. As we watch the battle of good and evil within the dying soul of George Firmin in Malcolm Lowry's *Under the Volcano*, we encounter Bill Plantagenet compounded of harrowed longing and hatred, of fathomless compunction and of remorse in *Lunar Caustic*.

They are representatives of people of the world who are in the throes of a crisis in their souls and thus Malcolm Lowry redeems the extreme subjectivism of his characters such as

1. *Ibid.*, pp. 303-304.

Bill Plantagenet by his contemplation of their predicament in a bigger perspective making them the dilemma of Everyman. Bill Plantagenet's stay at Bellevue is, no doubt, a voyage downward to "the foul core of his world"[1] but here too, in the person of Dr. Claggart is "the cure, wisdom and vision".[2] Bill Plantagenent has no doubt done irreparable damage to life by doing dirt on the holy impulses of life, the sacred bond of life but he is always haunted by remorse for the lack of graces of life in him.

This duality of vision is persistent in *Lunar Caustic* and saves it from becoming a tale of impressions loosely strung together. The narrator is not only content with giving subjective impressions of characters such as Bill Plantagenet, Garry and Kalowsky but he is there evaluating them with detachment. This detachment and objectivity is perceptible, when the narrator judges Bill Plantagenet's comradeship with his two friends Garry and Kalowsky shedding all illusions: "Part of the truth was that, like new boys in a hostile school, like sailors on their first long voyage on a miserable ship, like soldiers in a prison camp, they were drawn together in a doleful world where their daydreams mingled, and finding expression, jostled irresponsibly, yet with an underlying irreducible logic, around the subject of home-coming. Yet with them 'home' was never mentioned, save very obliquely by Garry. Plantagenet sometimes suspected the true nature of that miraculous day they looked to when their troubles would all be ended, but he coudn't give it away. Meanwhile it masqueraded before them in the hues of various dawns-never mind what was going to happen in its practical noontide".[3] The detachment manifest in this passage is a repudiation of the thinking that Malcolm Lowry's protagonist Bill Plantagenet is nothing but a literal transcript of his personal predicament.

This detached tone is not muted and muffled even in Bill Plantagenet, who is dismissed as a prey of delirium tremens,

1. *Ibid.*, p. 316.
2. *Ibid.*
3. *Ibid.*, p. 305.

incapable of taking detached view of things. Though Bill Plantagenet sees in Dr. Claggart some one working for the cure of patients at Bellevue, he does not hesitate to point out the futility of what the doctor is doing at Bellevue: "And he wondered if the doctor ever asked himself what point there was in adjusting poor lunatics to a mischievous world over which merely more subtle lunatics exerted almost supreme hegemony, where neurotic behaviour was the rule and there was nothing but hypocrisy to answer the flames of evil, which might be the flames of Judgment, which were already scorching nearer and nearer..."[1]

In a detached tone Bill Plantagenet says that hypocrisy has become the rule of life in the world and that people, who are themselves sunk in vile passions and are mad in their obsession with sordid materialism, are great dissemblers. They put on the veneer of righteousness and these people with their facade acting as a cover for their frenzy are subtle lunatics, sitting in judgement on poor lunatics who do not disguise themselves. Thus the dry ironic tone offers a scathing criticism of the rot that festers in the psyche of a man on account of dissimulation.

Dr. Claggart believes that the puppet show reminiscent of Robinson's expressionist film "Warming Shadows" in *Lunar Caustic* represents a definitely socializing influence, giving the patients an opportunity to get together and control their usual tendencies for emotional outbursts. But the detached tone of the narrator sums up its nullity: "Faces that had been intent for a time, however negatively, upon the antics of Caspar, collapsed in grey misery. At first there was a little speculation about the show: then not a nod "[2]

The puppet show is managed by a sane man from outside world but its impact on inmates of Bellevue hospital is pernicious, especially on Bill Plantagenet, who frightfully feels that his lot is no better than that of Caspar, dodging from one side of the stage to the other from the clutches of the giant.

1. Lowry, Malcolm: *Lunar Caustic*, pp. 316-17.

2. *Ibid.*, p. 317.

The experience is so searing that Bill Plantagenet feels driven friendless through hostile country into even darker corners, more remote hiding-places. The baneful result flowing from Dr. Claggart's mode of treatment is brought to the fore by ironic detachment. Dr. Claggart's pragmatism has its utility but it is too narrow and limited to grapple with the intensely human problem of inmates at Bellevue.

Its inadequacy lies in its utter disregard of the sensibility of persons living there and its readiness in imposing a regimen on all oblivious of their sensitivities. Thus the smothering of the individuality of inmates at Bellevue under Dr. Claggart's care makes Bill Plantagenet critical of Dr. Claggart's way of curing patients of their maladies: "I was also very jittery, but not too jittery to notice, after the excitement was over and we were being sweatily herded back, how each patient dropped back into his own world again, how senses that had thrilled to the game became numbed to stupor. It isn't difficult to see, therefore, why these should conform to the routine of the hospital, should do what they were told—since they waited to be told everything—even if that happened to be not to dare to take a shower before supper at all, or even, like the disciples, to wash their feet."[1]

This refusal of Bill Plantagenet to acquiesce into the harsh regimen of Dr. Claggart without any demur arises from the consistently ironic probing of Malcolm Lowry, who always looks at the two sides of the coin in *Lunar Caustic*. This divided vision of Malcolm Lowry enables him to make a continual inspection of the possibilities of his experience. Bellevue hospital is a microcosm of the diseased society of the world and Malcolm Lowry through its most articulate inmate Bill Plantagenet, makes an exploration of life and arranges diverse samples of life in an ordered pattern. At bottom are those for whom it is death-in-life. They are like T.S. Eliot's hollow men, "Shape without form, shade without colour, paralysed force, gesture without motion".[2]

1. Lowry, Malcolm: *Lunar Caustic*, p. 325.
2. Eliot, T.S.: *Selected Poems*, p. 77,

A vivid but sickening picture of life is evident in this passage from Malcolm Lowry's *Lunar Caustic*: "Later, when the nine high candles in their circular base were lighted above the old men who were considered too jittery or too obscene to eat with the others in the regular room, and they were bent over their stew in a grey, trembling despair, some seeming not to know they were eating at all, the food perhaps tasteless to them as they, cuffed it slowly and sleepily with their harmless spoons, others not even attempting to eat but wearing a fixed smile, as though the thought even of misery afforded them some perverse comfort. Plantagenet watching them, gradually thought he understood the meaning of death, not as a sudden, dispatch of violence, but as a function of life.[1]

All move wearily in a hideous procession round the words, looking at nothing, thinking of nolhing. They have neither the hope of heaven nor of hell. Most of the time with their heads bowed they walk in silence in that "marathon of the dead".[2] Kalowsky is such a man old, melancholy and small and feels resigned without any vestige of life in him: "We can only wait and see. So many things can happen in a life time".[3] It is very much akin to what T.S. Eliot says about life that wavers and fumbles in a dark hollow valley:

Between the desire.
And the spasm
Between the potency
And the existence
Between the essence
And the descent
Falls the shadow'.[4]

Apart from this awful prospect of death-in-life, life without praise or blame, is life that is knowingly evil, when Malcolm

1. Lowry, Malcolm: *Lunar Caustic*, p. 308.
2. *Ibid.*, p. 317.
3. *Ibid.*, p. 301.
4. Eliot, T.S., *Selected Poems*, p. 80.

Lowry says "on a tumbled blood-stained bed in a house whose face was blasted away a large scorpion was gravely raping a one-armed Negress".[1] The city of Newyork "...with the screaming of suicides, of girls tortured in hotels for transients, of people burning to death in vice dens, through all of which a thousand ambulances were screeching like trumpets"[2] is an appalling image of evil.

These are images of Inferno but *Lunar Caustic* which is Purgatorio, brings in other specimens of life in Bill Plantagenet, Garry and Battle. Bill Plantagenet is called Mr. Remorse, Garry a myth-maker and Battle, howsoever crazy, is an emblem of magnificent energy that goes to waste at Bellevue. It is Malcolm Lowry's technique in *Lunar Caustic* that puts the quick and the dead in an ordered pattern. It is difficult to agree with Douglas Day that Bill Plantagenet is "...another derelict in a city of derelicts".[3] Bill Plantagenet, who shudders at " . . . man's uncomplaining acceptance of his own degeneration" at Bellevue, is a character not insensitive to the claims of health and sanity. In the midst of the filthy, decaying and abandoned inmates, he shows the sign of redemption by contrition and remorse, when he screams: "But my god, it's horror . . . and all the fury, the anguish, the remorse, the voices, voices, voices, voices . . . pointing a solution, a way out into the morning light aad freedom . . ."[4] Malcolm Lowry works so dexterously that he gives us fleeting intimations of order and wholeness in Bill Plantagenet discernible in " . . . that part of him only a moment before in possession of the whole, the ship, was turning over with disunion of hull and masts uprooted falling across her decks . . ."[5]

Garry too stands out unique because of his sensitivity in the all-pervasive loathsome patient calm of Bellevue. If his stories are about things collapsing, falling apart, they are also about the innocent enjoyment of life and also about unrelenting ,

1. Lowry, Malcolm: *Lunar Caustic*, p. 299.
2. *Ibid*., p. 342.
3. Day, Douglas: *Molcolm Lowry: A Biography*, p. 210.
4. Lowry, Malcolm: *Lunar Caustic*, p. 334.
5. *Ibid*., p. 343.

fight with all setbacks in life. In Garry's stories about the impending doom lies his irrepressible desire for freedom from life-denying forces. The assertion of the simple and innocent delights of life is noticeable in his yearning for a journey to England so that he may see artists on the hillsides or cows and sheep-grazing in a green pasture or artists, painting pictures of flowers and the different birds and the mountains and the lakes and trees. Garry's story about the hunting of a whale recalls to mind the tenacity of Melville's Ahab on his whaling boat. Garry thus stands in a sharp contrast to gloom that appears to smother life at Bellevue. Malcolm Lowry's perception is so keen that he discovers the quintessence of life in Garry and puts it in relation to sterility under deceptive calm at Bellevue. Battle, too, and other negro sailors are also bursting with life and the song they make and their playing of the piano makes it clear that life is not extinct. All these are images of life and make a sad reflection on the futility of what Dr. Claggart is doing in the name of restoring health of patients at Bellevue.

Garry and Battle and other unnamed negro sailors sometimes work in unison with Bill Plantagenet and they take the bottom out of Dr. Claggart and make him vulnerable to the charge of shoving emblems of life into watertight compartments. The technique is such that Malcolm Lowry succeeds in mounting an assault on the seemingly sound system of Dr. Claggart, by showing a striking contrast between over-worked and exhausted, invariably adjustive and never existential Dr. Claggart, on the one hand and Bill Plantagenet, fighting a battle for his salvation within his psyche in the company of ebullient Garry and Battle, on the other.

Conrad Knickerbocker makes a very illuminating comment concerning Malcolm Lowry's technique in the Foreword to *Lunar Caustic*: "He often had five, ten or over twenty versions of a sentence, paragraph or chapter going at once. From these he selected the best, blending, annealing and reworking again and again to obtain the highly charged, multi-levelled style that characterises his writing".[1] This rigorous concern for

1. Knickerbocker, Conrad: Foreword to *Lunar Caustic*, p. 292.

form is proved by the painstaking manner involved in the making of *Lunar Caustic. Lunar Caustic* is the culmination of the process of annealing or conflation of a number of manuscripts, sometimes, appearing under the title "The Last Address" full of bitterness and sometimes, under the title "Swinging the Maelstrom" informed with an optimistic note. He is such a scrupulous writer that he compares one draft with the other and makes a fusion in a manner that a form emerges incarnating the vision he is trying to communicate. He appears to have the instinct of a Flaubert brooding over each word and sentence and a relentless reviser of his own writing.

This ever-alert reviser imparts a tight shape to *Lunar Caustic* that holds the density and depth of late works. *Lunar Caustic* is deeply allusive and this literary allusiveness consists in reference to Melville, Rimbaud and Dante. The allusiveness is a typical modern device in poetry, especially the poetry of T.S. Eliot. It is a laconic and terse juxtaposition of the splendour of experience embodied in the poetry of the past with the filth and squalor depicted in the poetry of the present time.

This juxtaposition lends a dramatic intensity to the work of art and it also adds a new dimension to the experience. Bill Plantagenet, moving from one saloon to the other, becomes Melville's Ahab "Stumbling from side to side on the careening bridge, feeling that he encompassed in his stare oceans from which might be revealed that phantom destroyer of himself'.[1] This affinity of Bill Plantagenet with Ahab gives a grandeur to Bill Plantagenet by recalling to mind Melville's "epic of the sea such as no man has equalled,"[2] and which "records, almost beyond pain or pleasure, the extreme transition of the isolated, far-driven soul, the soul which is now alone, without any real human contact".[3]

Bill Plantagenet has a feeling that he is all the time on the deck of a ship and once he gives his name as S.S. Lawhill to Dr. Claggart. He appears to be Melville who commands a

1. Lowry, Malcolm: *Lunar Caustic.*
2. Lawrence, D.H.: *Studies in Classic American Literature,* p. 151.
3. *Ibid.,* p. 139.

stillness in the soul, an awe, when he ceases to be American, when he forgets all audience and gives us his sheer apprehension of the word. Like Melville's Ahab, Bill Plantagenet wants to be the captain of his soul battling with the awful and infuriated whale.

Garry's stories have the curious symbolism of Rimbaud's poetry. This allusion to Rimbaud adds another rich texture to *Lunar Caustic*. To the outside world Garry appears to be a lunatic like Rimbaud but both Garry and his alter ego Rimbaud feel justified in having violent and apocalyptic visions. In his extraordinary masterpiece "Une Saison on Enfer" Rimbaud evokes a civilization shorn of religious faith, sunk in immorality and riven by war. Rimbaud feels himself the greatest accursed of people, dragging himself through stinking alleys and through this voyage into the abyss of himself, he wants to emerge purged and cleansed. Garry's mission is perhaps akin to that of Rimbaud and there is nothing degenerate about it. Graham Greene's characters too catch a glimpse of beautitude by journeying through inferno of their sordid passions.

The reference to Dante's purgatorio does not mean that Malcolm Lowry is writing an allegory. He writes a symbolist fable and not a sustained allegory. Purgatory is used to intimate the reader of the spiritual clime of the Lowry universe in *Lunar Caustic*. Its universe is not that of *Under the Volcano*, the inferno part of the sequence of seven novels *The Voyage that Never Ends*, Malcolm Lowry contemplates to write. In *Lunar Caustic* the hero is not only frightened of the evil that slumbers in him but he makes painful struggles to purge himself of grime. This literary allusiveness designed for giving a complex dimension to his experiences is taken to be "allusive cushioning" by Douglas Day. It is unfair on the part of Douglas Day to believe that the unadorned factual account of *Lunar Caustic* is too bitter a potion for him and consequently Malcolm Lowry feels the necessity of festooning it and this attempt at embellishment ends in obfuscation. The allusions to Rimbaud, Melville and Dante are mirrors on the tortured consciousness of Malcolm Lowry and are tools of effecting aesthetic distance.

It is a truism that Malcolm Lowry's equipment, such as it is, is subjective rather than objective, a better equipment, for a certain kind of poet than a novelist. The conception of *Lunar Caustic* is essentially poetical. This poetical conception of the novel is found in the profusion of images. At the outset of the novel the image that strikes the reader most is the image of a broken coal barge! "between the two wharves and fast against the poverty grass before the hospital lay the coal barge, sunken, abandoned, open, bull cracked, bollards adrift, tiller smashed, its hold still choked with coal dust, silt, and earth through which emerald shoots had sprouted".[1] This image recurs again in section VI of the novel. It is like recurrent motif that makes an evocation of the dissolution of life, the image of extinction. It is perhaps Malcolm Lowry's design-governing posture, giving the intimation of the shape of things we encounter at Bellevue. This image of decay and dissolution becomes the burden of the stories of Garry but in section X of the novel a new facet of life, couched in images of buoyancy comes to us. It is the image of a little children's fountain sending up a rainbow, an outspread peacock's fan of water, lovers resting for a while in some green niche of Paradise, lowers running for shelter, laughing, their arms round one another, even the riven trees with their crests in the sky yearning into the gloom, lit now by the heliotrope of lightning and the river below sparkling like ginger ale and seething with a million sequins. Bill Plantagenet feels a delicious sense of freedom, though this freedom is momentary.

Malcolm Lowry wants the reader to juxtapose the image of dissolution with the image of joy and life, knowing full well that joy is ephemeral. The very image of ruin in the coal barge, rotting in the river, sends emerald shoots, the emblem of life. To Lowry life consists in immedicable opposites defying all attempt at a resolution of the antinomies of life. Joy is momentary and it is the experience of wading through evil

1. Lowry, Malcolm: *Lunar Caustic*, p. 297.

that gives him an insight into reality. Bill Plantagenet has a fascination for the ragged man sitting motionless under the tree. He has a feeling that this ragged man knows the storm as the tree knows it. The storm is symbolic of outer as well as inner storm and Bill Plantagenet wants to have a mastery of the storm that rips through his psyche.

5

October Ferry to Gabriola

I looked to heaven, and tried to pray;
But or ever a prayer had gusht,
A wicked whisper came and made
My heart dry as dust.

—S.T. Coleridge, *The Ancient Mariner*

(A) DOMINANT THEMES

From a reading of Malcolm Lowry's *October Ferry to Gabriola* (1970) emerges the principal theme of evil in the psyche of man. The novelist shows the working of evil in all its terrifying form in Ethan Llewelyn, the protagonist of the novel. Ethan is a criminal lawyer of repute in the city of Toronto who chooses to retire from practice and after that he goes into retreat at Eridanus. The harrowing tale of evil works through Ethan Llewelyn's relationship with wife Jacqueline, Peter Cordwainer, an undergraduate mate of Ethan, a host of his clients and a fifteen-year-old Canadian youth Richard Chapman charged with making a criminal assault on a sixteen-year-old girl of his neighbourhood. Evil in the novel is existential in character revealing the very being of man. It has nothing to do with the social, economic and moral life of man. This discussion of evil is nothing but an inevitable product of a mind nourished by writers such as Dostoevsky,

William James and Jung. The discussion of evil, existential in nature, becomes overt, when Malcolm Lowry buttresses his ideas by making an allusion to Hermann Hesse's *Demian.*

The sentence of death served on Richard Chapman stirs the very being of Ethan and impels him to brood over evil of which Richard Chapman becomes a victim. Ethan's sympathies are with Richard Chapman and on account of his soft corner for a law-breaker in the eyes of jurymen a feeling may grow that Ethan is a pervert, because he takes the brief of an evil-doer. Malcolm Lowry's search is for assumptions underlying social, economic and moral dimensions of a man. The long excerpt from Hermann Hesse's *Demian* turns upside down the traditional moral touchstone apportioning praise on the righteous and blame on the vicious. He turns our gaze into the abyss of man and with clairvoyance enables us to see the murk and horror proliferating there. The abyss in the psyche abounds in savage passions which rip open the genteel veneer of respectability and Malcolm Lowry's assessment of Ethan is done on the basis of raw passions that rock a man's heart.

Hermann Hesse's intimate disclosures about the seamy side of his personality are germane to Lowry's interpretation of Ethan wallowing in mire. To Hermann Hesse, human psyche splits into two—the cosy and sheltered world that lofty and utopian ideals compose and the world of secret desires and passions. Malcolm Lowry feels that Hermann Hesse's awareness of two-fold life has an unerring rightness about it. The puritanical atmosphere in the family warps the naturalness of impulses and looks upon sex as a taboo. The sense of sex then comes to him as something forbidden, seduction and sin. The area of life then is strictly guarded against the corrupting power of sex.

Hermann Hesse has the experience of "guarded happiness"[1] in childhood. He lives under stern moral precepts sanctioned at home. The regimen of this life of moral vigour denies the existence of desires of a secret nature. The conscious self in him enjoins upon him the edifying talk of

1. Lowry, Malcolm: *October Ferry to Gabriola*, p. 268.

building a grand mansion upon the life of passions. Passions are volatile and shifting and the "new fabric"[1] erected by the conscious self is sure to crumble. Hermann Hesse finds that the imposing edifice of morality making for guarded happiness lies in ruins with the onrush of sensual passions.

It is the clash of the two, the strife between overpowering passions, on the one hand and the hard and brittle intellect, on the other. This war between passion and reason is the story of Everyman and if anyone claims that he is exempt from this inevitable clash of opposing selves, it is nothing but a hypocrisy. In the light of the tenor of reasoning as developed in Hermann Hesse, Malcolm Lowry flings the charge of hypocrisy in the face of jurymen pronouncing death sentence on Richard Chapman. Malcolm Lowry is of the view that if jurymen look into the abyss of their own selves at Chapman's age they too are sure to feel the overwhelming weight of passions.

His arguments rest on the assumption that there is not the slightest evidence to show that the boy is any way degenerate or vicious, on the contrary, we are told that the boy is quiet, a good boy. Malcolm Lowry says with a convincing defence of Richard Chapman. "For one thing is clear: a terrible thing like this would have happened to any one of us, the gentlemen of the jury themselves, yes, teven they themselves, when Chapman's age, might have perpetrated in all innocence what has been characterised and so sensationalised as an atrocity".[2] It has kinship with the disarming candour of Christ's persuasive counsel to self-styled guardians of morality stoning a woman caught in adultery in the New Testament, Christ's injunction to moralists to strip their own back is an exposure of the traditional moralists working in utter disregard of the compulsive course of passions in them.

Ethan Llewelyn's concern is not with what meets the eye on the surface but with the vehemence of passion refusing to acquiesce into moral stereotypes. Through Ethan's reflections

1. *Ibid.*
2. *Ibid.*, pp 267 68.

on the destiny of Richard Chapman on the scaffold, Malcolm Lowry develops the theme of evil vis-a-vis traditional ethic of life. The epithet "gentlemen" for members of jury awarding sentence of death on Richard Chapman is charged with irony. He means to say that jurymen gloat over their righteousness and with a shrug of their shoulders pass a damning judgement on Richard Chapman. An ethic which overlooks the elemental being of man and strives to make people fit into the procrustean bed of readymade morality is palpably inadequate.

Though Ethan is a lawyer, he speaks less in legal terminology and more in a philosophical language concerned with the basic impulsions of man. His is a descent into the inferno of vile passions of which conventional moralists are contemptuous and are afraid to stare them in the face. Ethan Llewelyn does not wear the blinkers of moral cliches, because he dares dive deep the pit of blood and mire and to clamber out of the pit with the horror he seizes there. It is, perhaps, a journey through the dark night of the soul. The landscape of Ethan's universe is pitch dark.

This theme of the dark night of the soul is evident from the two epigraphs one from George Eliot's *The Lifted Veil* and the other from Chaucer's *Troilus and Cressida* appended at the outset of the novel. The passage "There is no short cut, no patent tram road, to wisdom: after all the centuries of invention, the soul's path lies thorny wilderness which must be still trodden in solitude, with bleeding feet, with sobs for help, as it was trodden them of old time" has a bearing on the theme of evil in the novel.

The story of tasting the cup of sensual delight is not something new in Malcolm Lowry. It has a remote ancestry in the annals of literature, Marlowe's Doctor Faustus's soul thirsts after the pleasures of life. For the attainment of the cherished object of fleshly delights he enters into a pact with infernal powers and signs the bond with his own blood. He sells his soul for the sake of uninterrupted dalliance and at last reaps a harvest of nettles. Graham Greene's novels are peopled with characters who embrace evil by foregoing good in the beginning. Malcolm Lowry's characters in this respect take after Graham Greene's characters who reach after the grace of God by treading not the path of virtue, but the path paved with fire and brimstone. In the novel Jacqueline's perception of Ethan, a traveller through benighted landscape, is apt and throws sufficient light on the nature of theme with which the novelist is preoccupied; "But now she saw him as that very kind of man to whom great accidents happen—if fusion, it was also cumbustion—as a man who almost relished this, who, if he proposed to take her there at all, proposed to take her heaven by way of hell,..."[1] This journey to heaven by way of hell is also a favourite theme with Baudelaire. Baudelaire's experience of damnation has likeness with that of Malcolm Lowry and Graham Greene. The epigraph from Chaucer's *Troilus and Cressida* picturing man, all steerless within a boat amid the sea betwixt two winds that in contrary directions blow, sums up the theme of Ethan wrestling with evil in life. This strumggle with evil constitutes the nucleus of the novel.

Malcolm Lowry's earlier three novels *Ultramarine*, *Under the Volcano* and *Lunar Caustic* are also engaged with the problems of evil. The story of struggle with evil in these first three novels is keyed differently from his novel *October Ferry to Gabriola*. The going to heaven by way of hell is beset with odds at every step and the perception of love that redeems all is tenuous in them. Even a classic such as *Under the Volcano*, that has received acclaim at the hands of critics, has a weak grasp of the ineffable grace of life enlivening the relationship between the principal character Geoffrey Firmin and his wife Yvonne. In *October Ferry to Gabriola* Ethan Llewelyn is, no doubt, a man who proclaims that his life is blighted and his life is under a curse. He shows that he is capable of leading a life of great exaltation, though short-lived in the company of Jacqueline at Eridanus. The sensuousness he lavishes in a description of the unspoilt beauty of the virgin forest surrounding Eridanus testifies to his love of life. Malcolm Lowry does not invest George Firmin with such a

1. Lowry, Malcolm: *October Ferry to Gabriola*, pp. 106-7.

rich idiom suffused with delectable beauty in *Under the Volcano.* The rich tone of *October Ferry to Gabriola* is evident in this passage from the novel: "the perfume permeated partly by the scents of Jacqueline's spring flowers, but drawn out by spring showers and the blossoming trees in the depths of the forest, from wild cherry and wild crab apple and wood violet and wild rose there, as though the whole woods had undergone a saturation of perfume stronger than helliotrope or night-scented stock, at the same time nothing cleaner or fresher could be imagined, unless it was the salt sea smell of the inlet itself when it was running clear and pure".[1]

This exaltation of Ethan in the pure delightful images of life is evocative of a world quite unlike the world in *Under the Volcano* besmeared with darkness. In *Under the Volcano* Malcolm Lowry, in keeping with his design of creating the inferno segment of his *Drunken Divine Comedy*, show its protagonist Geoffrey Firmin perishing in awful barranca in the ignonimous company of a dog.

Thematically *October Ferry to Gabriola* is in a different key, because the gaze of the protagonist Ethan in it is not turned downward into the foul core of his world notwithstanding the fact that he is beset with forces impairing his hold on life. Ethan is also different from Malcolm Lowry's Dana Hilliot in *Ultramarine*, who too despite all attempts at finding a positive and harmonious commerce with the surrounding world, is seen looking into the abyss of his soul. Ethan feels obsessed with the guilt of goading his college friend at the University of Ely to take his own life. The guilt is like a foul toad in the cistern of his life. He is not at peace with himself because the feeling rankles in his mind that he is responsible for Peter Cordwainer's death. This preoccupation with guilt has no doubt an extremely harmful impact by engendering in him the sense of isolation from the community of mankind. He stands self condemned and looks upon himself as a pariah but the treatment of the theme of guilt in *October Ferry to Gabriola* is different from what Malcolm Lowry does of guilt in *Ultramarine* and *Under the Volcano.* In *October Ferry to Gabriola*

1. Lowry, Malcolm: *October Ferry to Gabriola*, pp. 157-58.

guilt generates in Ethan the intense desire for making penance, for making atonement for evil he has committed. Guilt in *October Ferry to Gabriola* has not the benumbing effect discernible in *Under the Volcano*. It is a consistent striving for the life of love, the life of faith transcending the tyranny of the self.

It is Ethan in *October Ferry to Gabriola* who is seen struggling hard, so that he may ascend to the loftier reaches of life. The section, *The Perilous Chapel* in *October Ferry to Gabriola* is central to the theme of the novel inasmuch as it embodies a tortuous search for reality, numinous in character, that may act as an epiphany for Ethan's guilt-ridden psyche, the point of illumination. It enables Ethan to perceive the essentials of life by jettisoning things that impede his ascension towards a meaningful life.

It is the life of faith powerfully expressed in terms of Ethan's encounter with the Roman Catholic priest on the deck of the ship bound for Gabriola. This incorporation of a whole section about faith vis-a-vis the carping consciousness of the individual is something new to the Lowry oeuvre. In novels such as *Ultramarine* and *Under the Volcano* protagonists make overture to the life of love to redeem themselves from the sordidness of life but the preponderant impression is not that of the sovereignty of love, it is rather the tyranny of the self that draws protagonists down into the murky caverns of their lives. In *October Ferry to Gabriola* the protagonist becomes aware of the utter futility of the tyranny of the self, he knows that sanity and peace come to soul only as a result of the effacement of the self and its merging in the bigger entity of God, who is nothing but love.

Ethan feels the overwhelming necessity of love in the midst of a life riven by doubt, uncertainty and guilt on top of everything. And his soul is so overpowered by the impulse to the life of faith that he makes a piteous supplication to the priest "—pay for me, Father."[1] Thus Ethan, beseeching the priest, wants to break off the Pact with the devil but this gesture for the benedictions of God meets with opposition in

1. Lowry, Malcolm: *October Ferry to Gabriola*, p. 303.

his mind from the tyranny of self: "I don't know Father. I'not sure I really want you to really pray for me. It's for others. Many others."[1] Ethan feels the imperative of heavenly love giving certitude to the vexations of his spirit but his preoccupation with the life of guilt interposes a barrier between himself and the supervening grace of God. This is nothing but duplicity in a character who craves for the grace of God in one moment and in the other makes a disclaimer that he has no such yearning for faith. This duality is characteristic of Dana Hilliot in *Ultramarine* and Geoffrey Firmin in *Under the Volcano*. But this duality assumes a new dimension in *October Ferry to Gabriola*, when its protagonist Ethan moves towards a measure of acceptance of life in its essential forms without any attempt at putting a gloss over it. The dissimulation with which Ethan covers his self, falls like a pack of cards and his soul writhing, in anguish stands naked before us: "I feel like a hypocrite. All I know is I want passionately to want not to be a hypocrite".[2] All defences of Ethan crumble and he is deeply touched by the priest's injunction that salvation lies in the naivete of childhood, when the rational and sceptic mind is in abeyance. From the priest Ethan learns the secret of peace by letting the fire of baptism pass through him and consuming his self battered by doubt and guilt.

In *October Ferry to Gabriola*, Malcolm Lowry has found a character in Ethan who is on the right side of despair, unlike the character of Bill Plantagenet in *Lunar Caustic*, tumbling into despair notwithstanding his search for faith. This wrestling with despair does not leave Ethan maimed and battered, because he shows for the first time in his long travail the sign of being in tune with his destiny and that of the universe: "It was true that if you suffered long enough and died enough and defied any event completely to cut you down, in the end everything could change very suddenly. Then, just as he'd seemed on the brink of complete despair, the priest had supplied him with a measure of reassurance, indeed a kind of goal. Should they establish themselves on Gabriola, Ethan would

1. Lowry, Malcolm: *October Ferry to Gabriola*, p. 304.
2. *Ibid.*, pp. 306-307.

visit him, would visit his chapel, would discuss his problems, and Jacqueline's problems, and their problems. Never had Ethan felt more in need of advice from an older man, be he priest or no. And with this reassurance the priest had given him Ethan found he had attained too, on the sudden, a measure of acceptance."[1]

This quest for faith is a prop bolstering the protagonist trembling with despair on the edge of a precipice and this finds an expression in Ethan's powerful apprehension of a mysterious order above the mundane world of ours. The compulsive course of the divine supernatural order affecting the destiny of man finds a powerful evocation here: "...on our journey through life, some guardian spirit causes our attention to be drawn, at such moments, to certain combinations, whether of events, or persons or things, but which we recognise, as speaking to us in a secret language, to remind us that we are not altogether unwatched, and so encourage us to our highest endeavour, and especially is this true, when we most neeed help, which is almost the same as saying when we most need assurance that our lives are not valueless...?...if it is not God, or of God, this eye that hears, this voice that thinks, this heart that speaks, this embodied hallucination that foresees with more than crystal clarity, and divine speech."[2]

This conception of an order inexplicable and inscrutable watching and controlling the affairs of men is nothing but numinous and in view of this supervening world of the supernatural Ethan implores the priest of the Perilous Chapel of Gabriola to make prayer for his soul. The consciousness of civilized man feels out of tune with this divine supernatural order. For its appreciation is needed a primitive method of thinking the consciousness of civilized men has largely discarded. Malcolm Lowry through his protagonist Ethan in *October Ferry to Gabriola* develops the theme of the supernatural as a counterpoint to the civilized consciousness of men resulting in his ruination. It is a syncopation of two diverse

1. Lowry, Malcolm: *October Ferry to Gabriola*, pp. 306-307.
2. *Ibid.*, p. 320.

worlds, one living by reason and the other by spirit. This world of the spirit sometimes comes to us in the form of the irrational.

The inexplicable outbreak of fire recurring at places in the novel burning many a house, including Ethan's house Barkerulle is an instance of the irrational. No specific cause of fire has been identified. It is supposed that fire results from the preponderance of evil in the world. The atmosphere is so thick with evil that there is internal combustion, ignition without any palpable cause. The film *The Wandering Jew* Ethan witnesses is also the story of fire that works mysteriously. It all appears to be an affair of the occult and the irrational in the vein of Yeats's *A Vision* but in the Lowry universe the occult and the irrational have been woven into the psychological reality of characters: "In no time at all one had been pleasantly convinced that certain unexplained fires (apart from those that seemed the undoubted work of poltergeists whatever they, finally, were) had actually been feared into existence: that on occasion, feelings of sheer hatred or revenge toward other human beings had been sufficient to cause, without admixture of purposive "magic", disaster, otherwise inexplicable, to others."[1]

Thus one of the major themes of *October Ferry to Gabriola* inheres in the interrelationship of the psychic, the occult and the supernatural in life. This integrated vision may not find a sustained development in the character of Ethan but Ethan feels that human life is surrounded by an area of darkness where imponderables wallow and flounder. This attempt at the synthesising of the disparate forces working inside man and forces operating outside man makes *October Ferry to Gabriola* a novel richer in kind than the preceding ones. Thus Ethan who is shown striving after the life of faith after the harrowing journey through the vale of doubt and guilt nostalgically recalls to mind the prayer he has been taught as a child: "Grant me, oh Lord, to know that which is worth knowing, to love that which is worth loving, to praise that which pleaseth thee most, to esteem that highly which to

1. Lowry, Malcolm: *October Ferry to Gabriola*, p. 139.

Thee is precious, to abhor that which in Thy sight is filthy and unclean."[1] The craving for abounding love the prayer recaptures is a longing for the burial of the self tainted by evil and resurrection of the innocence and naivete of childhood. It is the idea of divine dispensation that makes Ethan treat his eviction from Eridanus as a will of God: "So he must try to accept this as the working of a higher will, of God's will? For Eridanus, and the healing peace it had brought him, had come almost like a gift from God, and what that life was, in reality, and in its beauty, could never perhaps be lost..."[2]

Closely allied with the theme of faith in a supernatural order coming as a redeeming agent for soul sunk in despair is the theme of love in a pilgrim soul taking everything in its stride. It is love that subsists between Ethan and Jacqueline in course of their stay at Eridanus makes them feel that they have attained felicity. Malcolm Lowry speaks of their ecstatic life at Eridanus in an intensely charged vein: ... "they enjoyed almost complete freedom and privacy, peace and quiet, they swam and sun-bathed, and if they wanted to sing at the tops of their voices at four o'clock in the morning, or Ethan play the clarinet wildly as the early Ted Lewis himself—it was the flute in Virgil's Eclogues—no one would hear them, save may be a heron croaking eerily by on some moonlit fishing trip."[3]

This life of supreme happiness gets a severe jolt, when the threat of eviction from Eridanus comes from Harbour Board Authorities. The shack Ethan and Jacqueline have built with loving care at Dollarton bears testimony to their mutual abounding love in the face of their being vulnerable to the perilous onslaughts of the sea. The proposed eviction of Ethan from Eridanus, the land of his heart's desire, is no doubt a cause of excruciating pain to him but he has the soul of a pilgrim who has the readiness to embark on the ark of life in the troubled waters of the sea of life. The life at Eradinus with its healing peace is no doubt a gift from God but he knows the

1. Lowry, Malcolm: *October Ferry to Gabriola*, p. 295.
2. *Ibid.*
3. *Ibid.*, pp. 62-63.

reality that life lies in its protean change. In keeping with this ever changing conception of life Ethan makes the declaration that he doesn't hesitate relinquishing the incomparable beauty of Eridanus.

This readiness on the part of Ethan to launch himself into life without shedding tears for lost love speaks of the deep roots ingrained in him: "And what would the cabin and their life on the beach have been without Jacqueline's love, the love she put into it? To remain attached to the place as property, which in aany case it was not (unless a few to-by-force, and nails, a well)—he thought, looking at the planks askew on the poop, seemed blasphemy."[1] Ethan and his wife Jacqueline are like two young lovers newly married in D.W. Griffith's *Isn't Life Wonderful*. Though the lovers are driven from their home by bandits with their parents killed and their huts set to fire, and these two defenceless lovers are lost in the forest and despair is writ large on their face, they don't give way to despair and gaze up with a hungry supplication at wild beauty of trees and stormy moonlight above them.

Ethan and Jacqueline are like Griffith's lover enchanted by the poetry of the earth which knows no death. They are perhaps imbued with what the novelist says at one place in the novel. "Suddenly death appeared an enemy, the world so different from the earth, not less so: then you were a great deal stronger than death too, if you had love, and faith in that love."[2] This conception of love does not treat life as a cloistered shell from which is absent the disagreeable in experience. Ethan knows that reality is in a state of flux. It is dynamic and protean and we have to be in tune with this continuous change which is the quintessence of life. Ethan knows that his paradise in the form of Eridanus is about to crumble but he doesn't sulk over it, because he knows how to go the whole hog. In a passionate discourse with Jacqueline he looks at life in all its changing phases good and bad: "Perhaps it's something like a sunrise: when it's at its very best you say, oh, if it would just stay like that forever, but if

1. Lowry, Malcolm: *October Ferry to Gabriola*, p. 295.
2. *Ibid.*, p. 17.

it did you'd never know what full noon was like, or midnight either. No, it was time to leave, however much it hurts."[1] Ethan's Eridanus is not Thoreau's blissful state of concord. Lowry's Eridanus imagined by Ethan, the protagonist of *October Ferry to Gabriola,* is a blend of joy and sorrow. His Eridanus engenders corruption from within and it is love which is the sole weapon to fight forces that deny life.

The theme of love thus developed in *October Ferry to Gabriola* "...involves a dying away of the old self into a more authentic mode of being where one discovers the myth he must render into life."[2] Ethan's landing on the island of Gabriola involves a break with the past with all its attendant guilt and sickness in the soul and the beginning of a new life. Though there is not the tempting spectacle of the splendour of gold and scarlet maples of the days of Eridanus about Gabriola, it has a "...splendour of blackness, of darkness".[3] The island of Gabriola looks wild, lonely primeval and forbidding but underneath this awful exterior lies the irrepressible impulse to life. The impulse to life and love is indestructible, because it finds its manifestation in some one burning tree stumps to clear his land and a voice calling out clear across the water to Ethan and Jacqueline to Gabriola. Ethan and Jacqueline are not daunted in the least by the sullen prospect Gabriola offers and they are seen walking "...along the beach in the stinging cold salt air."[4] This haunting sense of love comes to the rescue of Ethan whose soul is sold to the devil and who is sick to death.

The growing inroads of the industrial civilization into the preserve of nature also make an assault on the bastion of love in the heart of a man. Malcolm Lowry in *October Ferry to Gabriola* shows the pernicious effect of industrialization on the wholesome rhythms of life, when he talks about Shellco refinery at Vancouver. The baneful impact is shown vividly by the olfactory contrast between colossal stench arising from the

1. Lowry, Malcolm: *October Ferry to Gabriola*, p. 325.
2. Cross, K. Richard: *Malcolm Lowry*, p. 106.
3. Lowry, Malcolm: *October Ferry to Gabriola*, p. 332.
4. *Ibid*., p. 331.

gruesome carpet of dirty oil spreading everywhere on the surface of the sea and the blast of heavenly fragrance wafted from the forest. At first Shellco appears to be quiet and unobtrusive but it fastens its tentacles all over the landscape as if it were a monster A shiver runs down the spine of Ethan, when 'fiendish lurid light',[1] comes from the whole refinery. The magnificent din appears to be hellish and from the oil waste pyre comes wishing, whistling consistent rushing roar, mingling with a noise like rattling giant's chains.

The menace the industrialization poses to life has been profoundly felt by Ethan in *October Ferry to Gabriola* and has been rendered with the sensitiveness of D.H. Lawrence. The clash of the life styles of two opposed modes of being, one the life of primeval innocence and the other the life of soullessness, evident in industrialization. In the name of modernity and industrialization the healthy rhythms of life Ethan and Jacqueline experience in the immediacy of eternity by which they are surrounded and nursed at Eridanus, and where antiquity of mountains, forest and sea conspire on every hand to reassure and protect them is smothered and hideous houses spring up in place of old houses of fishermen with distinctiveness about them.

The indiscriminate coming up of a number of soulless houses finds a severe indictment here: "But everywhere else, it seemed, the shingled houses were falling like ninepins, each day cupolas tumbled off the poor old steamboat Gothic buildings being torn down, like the trees, to make way for more soulless Behemoths in the shape of hideous new apartment buildings yet more deathscapes of the future."[2] The soullessness that comes in the wake of industrialization is also noticeable in the colour scheme of buildings that spring up. The Ocean Spray Inn looks abominable on account of its awful colour scheme. Ethan and Jacqueline turn their nose at ugliness created by the colours of the inn that appear to have been brewed, perhaps in some infernal cauldron. The colours create an ugliness the world had not

1. Lowry, Malcolm: *October Ferry to Gabriola*, p. 159.
2. *Ibid.*, p. 177.

thought of before. The room of the inn appears to be perfect outward expression of its own inner soul full of despair and ennui. The novelist creates the repulsive and macabre life at Ocean Spray Inn: "The light turned the denizens of the place into corpses, their flesh a yellowish grey, with purple lips and cheeks. Near the lavatory under a neon cerise floodlight, something sat in the corner; a sack, it looked like, under those macabre lights; not a sack, it was square, more like a wardrobe, and draped with a spotted filthy wrinkled grey canvas under these cerise ceiling lights that glared down like three pairs of mechanical eyes. And the carpet, for there was a carpet, seemed to be composed of some sort of evil fungus, in which growths struggled with each other, ash-colored and slime black. The windows were either boarded up, like those of prisons, he thought, in the citadel of Parma,..."[1] In the manner of D.H. Lawrence Ethan feels that we pay a heavy price in terms of the desolation of spirit for progress. The inordinate greed and avarice in tearing up treasures from the bowels of the earth in course of hectic industrialization is soul-killing. The plundering of nature recoils on man: "There was this Hofmannsthal or Broch—who said nature had been tamed and the terror had gone into the cities".[2] Thus the terror that grips people in cities results from industrialization and Malcolm Lowry through Ethan makes a severe deprecation of industrial life. The feverish pace of industrialization spreads the germ of its disease all over the sylvan landscape evident in the indiscriminate felling of trees and the fire hazard created by the loggers who leave huge logged-off areas uncleared and inflammable brush. The havoc wrought by man in plundering nature receives scating criticism at the hands of Ethan. Ethan's abhorrence mounts when he finds people desecrating the forest: "As far as the eye would reach there seemed whole mountain sides of burned and dead trees, whole forest that looked as though they would never grow again. The abomination of desolation sitting in a holy place.... Man makes the mistake of thinking that because life is so prodigal in

1. *Ibid.*, p. 257.
2. *Ibid.*, p. 223.

expenditure of itself that its resources are everywhere inexhaustible and that there is no such thing as death without rebirth."[1]

Ethan feels that rebirth is possible, when he makes himself at one with the elemental rhythms of nature not yet sullied by the ravenous hunger of man. Malcolm Lowry whose voice speaks through Ethan in *October Ferry to Gabriola* emphasizing the salutary effect of the sacred bond between man and nature himself says about it in *The Forest Path to the Spring*. The rapport between man and nature essential for the wellbeing of man finds a remarkable expression in the opera *The Forest Path to the Spring*. "And suddenly, as I helped my wife out and tied up the boat, I was overwhelmed with a kind of love. Standing there, in defiance of eternity, and yet as if in humble answer to it with their weathered sidings as much a part of the natural surroundings as a Shinto temple is of the Japanese landscape, why had these shacks come to represent something to one of indefinable goodhess, even a kind of greatness? And some shadow of the truth that was later to come to me, seemed to steal over my soul, the feeling of something that man had lost, of which these shacks and cabins, brave against the elements but at the mercy of the destroyer, were the helpless yet stalwart symbol, of man's hunger and need for beauty, for the stars and the sunrise."[2] This hunger and need for the beauty of nature, not yet despoiled by man's inordinate greed for treasure, is one of the basic themes of *October Ferry to Gabriola*. This sensitivity to the romance that nature proffers to man will enable Ethan shattered by guilt and despair to rise from his ashes like a phoenix clapping its wings. This yearning for the resurrection of the soul sick to death by an immersion in the delightful rhythms of nature is not to be found in his novel *Under the Volcano*. In one of his letters to Albert Erskine Malcolm Lowry says that in course of the composition of *October Ferry to Gabriola* his spiritual position is worse than that of Dante when he composes Inferno. He is faced

1. *Ibid.*, p. 217.
2. *Ibid*, pp. 233-34.

with a big challenge not to his sanity or otherwise but with the vital problem of life death and rebirth. Rebirth, now liberation from bondage to despair lies in his close habitation with the elemental powers beautifully summed up in sections Eridanus and The Tides of Eridanus in *October Ferry to Gabriola*.

(B) ART OF CHARACTERISATION

Iris Murdoch in her essay *The Sublime and the Beautiful Revisited* observes: "When we think of the works of Tolstoy or George Eliot, we are not remembering Tolstoy and George Eliot, we are remembering Dolly, Kitty, Stiva, Dorothea and Casaubon".[1] But when we come to a modern novelist such as Malcolm Lowry we find him writing in a letter to Albert Erskine that "Character-drawing is virtually non-existent"[2] in his nevel *October Ferry to Gabriola*. In the case of Tolstoy and George Eliot who belong to the central tradition of realist novelists the values of life are stable.

When values are well defined in life and are taken for granted, novelists create characters who are autonomous and vibrant centres of life but in the case of modern novelists of whom Malcolm Lowry is one there is a retreat from character. This retreat from character is on account of the absence of stable values in life. A modern novelist is haunted by a sense of increasing alienation, he is tormented by radical doubts about the nature of reality.

We are no longer certain of the world we live in; Physics, Psychology, Politics and Philosophy all conspire to dissolve the comfortably social boundaries of our everyday world. Reality becomes flickering and evanascent and when a novelist of our times wants to picture these fleeting nuances of life, he finds it difficult to delineate characters as realists like Tolstoy and George Eliot do. Of this everchanging reality, Ethan, the protagonist in Malcolm Lowry's *October Ferry to*

1. *The Sublime and the Beautiful Revisited*, Yale Review Volume 49, 1959, p. 226.

2. Lowry, Malcolm: *Selected Letters*, p. 239.

Gabriola, feelingly speaks: "A novelist presents less of life the more closely he approaches what he thinks of as his realism. Not that there were no plots in life, nor that he could not see a pattern, but that man was constantly in flux, and constantly changing. He woke up a Buddhist, was a Catholic at breakfast, a Hater of Life with the morning paper, and then a Protestant, and then by the time he got to the library was something else,—."[1]

Malcolm Lowry's concern is thus with the highly volatile state of mind of his protagonist. He perhaps belongs to the tradition inaugurated by Richardson and culminating in Conrad and Henry James exploring beneath the surface appearance of things, moving towards subterranean areas of experience.

Notwithstanding Malcolm Lowry's disclaimer that character-drawing is non-existent in *October Ferry to Gabriola* he goes deep into the psyche of Ethan, the protagonist of the novel and with great delicacy and discrimination shows the unrest that is brewing there. Each tremor in his heart is recorded with great fidelity, every struggle Ethan makes to clamber out of the abyss of fear and hatred is graphically rendered in an evocative language. Thus character-drawing is there in a subtle and delicate way indistinguishable from the other elements of the novel such as the narrative mode, plot, diction and moral vision. A good novel is not studied exclusively in terms of either character or plot-construction or its moral content. All the diverse constituents simultaneously fuse and incarnate the vision of which character is only one essential element.

Characters in *October Ferry to Gabriola* may be put in a number of groups. The members of different groups interact with one another and produce the unity of impression. The first group is composed of characters such as Ethan, his wife Jacqueline and their son Tommy. The novel *October Ferry to Gabriola* is the story of love and discord between Ethan and Jacqueline who are the principal characters round whom all

1. Lowry, Malcolm: *October Ferry to Gabriola*, p. 61.

other characters in the novel move. Their son Tommy has a brief spell in the life of the couple in the novel. In the second category comes the father of Ethan who is more or less a character in the background in the first few chapters of the novel. The relationship between Ethan and his father is quite unhappy. Ethan's disdainful attitude to his father is from the very outset of the novel. To Ethan the father is a source of tension.

In the third category comes Peter Cordwainer who is Ethan's collegemate at the University of Ely. Peter Cordwainer too appears in a few snatches of conversation with his collegemate Ethan. Though Peter Cordwainer appears quite briefly in the novel, he is an obsession with Ethan. Ethan feels that he is accountable for Peter Cordwainer's death and he cannot rid himself of the guilt arising from his accountability for Peter Cordwainer's death.

The fourth group is composed of Angus Mc Candless, the father of Jacqueline and his mistress Flora Mc Clintock. Angus is perhaps Ethan's split-self or doppelganger. Angus's interest in the esoteric cult of Cabbalism has something to do with Ethan's interest in occult powers. The fifth group has its sole member in the Catholic priest of the Perilous Chapel of Gabriola. The priest too is vitally connected with Ethan in dire need of faith in a mysterious order giving meaning and coherence to life. Apart from these human characters is the character of place and its milieu. As Wessex becomes a live character in a Hardy novel, Eridanus becomes a powerful entity shaping Ethan and his relationship with his wife Jacqueline. It is not only Eridanus but the entire landscape of Toronto and Vancouver that broods over the destiny of Ethan in the manner of landscape in a Hardy novel.

Ethan Llewelyn is born in Ontario. When he is two he leaves Canada and returns to it until he is twenty-two. This long spell of absence from the place of his nativity goes against him. It engenders in him the galling sense of isolation from the main stream of Canadian life. Ethan says "Everybody takes me for an Englishman and they seem to hate the English like the devil."[1] This feeling of loneliness in Ethan is accentuated by the indifference of his parents to him in his boyhood. The only kind of loving action Ethan recalls on the part of either of his parents is the gift of a beautiful toy-model of Moscow to him. When Ethan's father in the last year of peace before the First World War is a legal adviser on international cotton law in Czarist Russia, he brings back to his son a beautiful replica of the magic bulbar city of Moscow.

Ethan goes ecstatic over the toy-model but his happiness is quite short-lived, because the gift is callously taken back from him. Ethan is too afraid of the father to ask for the toy model of Moscow later. Thus from his very childhood Ethan has the feeling of being a castaway, a derelict for whom there is none to care. Speaking of his wretched childhood Ethan says that his father sends him away year after year to prep school—a boarding school in Stoke-Newington where he is not allowed to do any work or play any games and he wanders about the grounds in dark glasses or a double eye shade or one eyeshade because he suffers from corneal ulceration.

Ethan also recalls being kept in a state of semi-starvation. He considers it to be a stroke of good luck, when he sees an egg and a glass of milk in a month. The fact that pinches Ethan most is that he has not received "any treatment for his eyes beyond zinc ointment castor oil, and a flogging, when he had a relapse from a junior master—".[2] When Ethan is home for holidays, the father prefers to beat his chilblains with a razor strop and insisting at the same time that his certain dirty school-boy-habits which have already led to complete impoverishment of his blood would result in atophy and complete idiocy and finally death at the age of nineteen. In a tone of indignation Ethan says that his father does not take him to an eye specialist, until he is thirteen and when he finally takes him to a London Ophthalmologist who puts

1. Lowry, Malolm: *October Ferry to Gabriola*, p. 13.
2. *Ibid.*, pp. 22-23.

Cocaine on his eyes and "simply scraped the affliction away in half-an-hour like a sailor scraping rust off a deck."[1]

Ethan piles up all these details showing that alienation from his father is complete. This alienation from the fount of love a child drinks at in the family deals a shattering blow to Ethan from which he wants to recover all through the novel. The grievous loss of parental affection causing a severe wound in the psyche of Ethan is further compounded, as time goes by. Ethan's agony increases all the more, when he finds Barkerville, the family mansion he has moved into after his father's death, is reduced to ashes. He is seized with the feeling that he doesn't deserve the parental house. He has the sense of being an unworthy heir of the family house and taken the fire that destroys the house in May 1946 as the sign of his damnation. This sense of damnation is further deepened when the memory of his dead friend Peter Cordwainer unnerves him beyond any repair. He feels unhinged when he holds himself accountable for Peter Cordwainer's death. All these selective details bring the idea home to us and Ethan is sick to death, he is a soul sold to infernal powers. He has the awful feeling of being situated in a chaotic limbo at the very outermost fringes of the world feeling lonely and homeless, feeling himself so cut off: ". . . he had always remained half-conscious of his isolation from his fellowmen. He'd tended to see people groups, integrated among themselves, excluding him—See— that fellow sitting over there in the corner, I'm not sure I like the shifty look of him, he is not one of us,—".[2]

In this agonising predicament resulting from isolation he finds Jacqueline who too has a similar anguish in her soul. Jacqueline, the daughter of Angus Mc Candless, has a wretched childhoold like Ethan. Jacqueline's mother, the mistress of Angus Mc Candless abandons her at Mc Candless' door-step in freezing January night in Winnepeg, when she is a week child. With a sense of shame Jacqueline tells Ethan that she is the bastard child of Angus Mc Candless. The fact of homelessness coupled with shame shakes Jacqueline to her foundations and makes her feel cut adrift from her

1. *Ibid*, p. 23.
2. *Ibid*, p. 43.

moorings: "... Jacqueline's parents had come to live mostly apart so she no longer had a "home"...."[1] Ethan and Jacqueline suffer from a crisis in their souls and are thus denizens of the same spiritual clime. However, in a subtle manner they differ in their perspectives on life and Malcolm Lowry appears to be very deft in making subtle delineations of differences in the character of the two.

Character-creation in *October Ferry to Gabriola* is not to be seen in terms of characters as autonomous entities but in terms of a complicated structure of human relationship. Jacqueline is "slim and supple, dark-haired, and incredibly young and passionate looking—...."[2] We further learn that Jacqueline "Prided herself on her independence, went everywhere unescorted if she felt like it, was a chain smoker, liked to drink gin and orange juice, loved good movies and taught school in an Ontario village: music, French, botany, literature everything, ..."[3] We further gather from Jacqueline that she has never caught on to any religion and her father has counselled her never to give over her will into the hands of another power.

All these details strengthen the belief that Jacqueline is a free spirit forging her way on her own. The crisis in her soul generates in her a craving for some prop on which to rest and in this quest for stay in life she comes to Ethan and marries him. But she also wants to rid herself of dependence: "her womanliness craved dependence on Ethan even while wanting to free herself from its tyranny."[4]

This duality in Jacqueline presages that her relationship with Ethan will be under strain. Jacqueline's marriage with Ethan is bound to be unhappy, because both have different expectations from each other. Jacqueline feels drawn to Ethan "by the poseur the actor, who had won her with her likeableness, his good looks, humour, his air of success, his success-

1. *Ibid* , p. 30.
2. *Ibid.*, p. 12.
3. *Ibid.*
4. *Ibid.*, p. 107.

itself, and everyday sense of adventure."[1] In course of living her life with Ethan she discovers to her dismay that underneath the poseur and the veneer of likeableness in Ethan, is a man who is like her father; ". . . a man almost without worldly ambition in the usual sense, who, seeing life's very meaning as an ordeal perhaps feeling man's purpose on earth at all simply going through the hoop, had already accepted the fire as some necessary expiation;. . . ."[2]

Thus on the surface the two characters Ethan and Jacequeline share loneliness principally on account of their wretched childhood but in reality they are poles apart: "...it was life, their life, their marriage aborted in its rebirth so miserably by the fire, and now found wanting or in the balance."[3] They are also unhappy on the score of their son Tommy who is always away from home. Ethan's remark about Tommy "To hell with Tommy, for the moment!" cuts Jacqueline to the Enick who in an injured tone retorts "what! would you like him to grow up feeling as you did about your father?"[4] Thus Ethan and Jacqueline are locked in an internecine warfare. The former is obsessed with guilt and expiation and looks upon life as a penetentiary and the latter refuses to see life in terms of an ordeal as she wants the obvious from life and has little to do with damnation and redemption of soul. When Jacqueline wants to know from Ethan if he will say *Isn't Life Wonderful*? when they are driven out into a forest with everything gone away, he feels sorrowful and hopcless and in a tone of despair says, "But I'm too old for you."[5]

Malcolm Lowry has here an ironic conception of the two characters—one seeking to relish the best of life and the other sliding slowly into the slough of despondency. Jacqueline doesn't want to do anything that threatens to be tragic, she doesn't want a repetition of disgraceful circumstances of her own birth. She is mortally afraid of the fear of repeating the

1. *Ibid* , p. 106.
2. *Ibid.*, p. 106.
3. *Ibid.*, p. 106.
4. *Ibid.*, p. 105.
5. *Ibid.*, p. 18.

cycle of her mother, of going insane herself, facing the pathetic business of being a foundling too, a bloody bastard picked up on a door-step. The divided loyalties of love and hatred of home, longing for and hatred of respectability is gnawing at her soul. Jacqueline's desire for a life of love is thwarted, because she has to live with Ethan whose life is gripped by fear and guilt: "And out of the fears grew wild hatreds, great unreasoning esemplastic hatreds: hatred of people who looked at him so strangely in the street; long forgotten hatreds of schoolmates who'd persecuted him about his eyes at school; hatred of the day that ever gave him birth to be the suffering creature he was, hatred of a world where your houses burned down with no reason, hatred of himself, and out of all this hatred did not grow sleep."[1]

Hatred and guilt are so powerful that when he sees the movie *The Wandering Jew* he discovers in the jew his own symbolic projection. The dreadful story of the poor jew cursed by Christ never to die through the centuries is nothing but the predicament of Ethan. Like the jew Ethan has a longing for death but death eludes Ethan. It is a tormenting state of mind. Thus as a novelist of the inner working of the mind Malcolm Lowry is superb. It is a dramatization of the coming together of Ethan and Jacqueline in the hope of celebrating the poetry of the earth but to their dismay they meet with deception and tragedy.

Jacqueline's father Mc Candless who has the gift of prescience is not taken in by the seemingly happy life of Ethan and Jacqueline at Eridanus and he rightly has a premonition of pitfalls, lurking in their relationship: "Nor that, for his part, during his stay, he probably meant to impugn their precious beach life. His point seemed to be, as if that new life involved a task he'd magically conjured up for them himself, their own attitude was one in question. For him Eridanus apparently wasn't a place to be enjoyed, so much as another test of their love, to be endured heroically, come through."[2] Mc Candless looks upon himself as Prospero and

1. *Ibid*, p. 124.
2. *Ibid.*, p. 155.

considers Ethan and Jacqueline to be Ferdinand and Miranda respectively in Shakespeare's *The Tempest.*

Malcolm Lowry through the allusion of Ferdinand and Miranda develops a positive norm of life, a life of love and trust against the backdrop of a life of travail. Ethan and Jacqueline fail in their test of love by the yardstick of abounding love subsisting between Ferdinand and Miranda. Mc Candless and Flora Mc Clintock are a foil to Ethan and Jacqueline. Mc Candless and Flora Mc Clintock are cards, characters who are flat in E.M. Forster's sense of the term but they stand in a sharp contrast to the round and developing characters of Ethan and Jacqueline. Malcolm Lowry's character-creation is here working in an unobtrusive manner by asking the reader to juxtapose characters with varying perspectives on life.

Mc Candless takes life with a remarkable zest and with great exaltation forges ahead surmounting all odds. In Mc Candless's life ordeals are many but he is not Ethan who becomes a lame duck and despairs and seeks a sanctuary nursing his sorrows. Mc Candless keeps on changing vocation after vocation and he considers his change of calling to be a retreat but it is not the retreat of Ethan because every retreat involves seriousness on his part in girding up his loins. Recounting the sage of his life Mc Candless says "In this country I started at eight dollars a month in 1905 on a Stock farm working from daylight to dark. There was a retreat for you... The following year I got forty dollars a month breaking horses on a ranch in Saskatchewan. Then I rode herd on Toodoggone River Ranch for twenty-five dollars a month and board. That's two more retreats. In 1908 I took up a homestead sixty miles from Dumble, Alberta, I sold that for twenty dollars an acre after three years homestead duties, which was worse, on the whole, than the Montesquieu Letters. I went overseas in 1914, more in pity than in anger still faithful to Old England—the most unusual bloody retreat of the lot... I was invalided home with a leg wound in November 1917 and in February 1919 I bought a poultry farm of Onion Lake, where I lost heavily on account of the low price of eggs."[1] Mc Candless takes everything in his stride and "thought of nothing else but the great "Plan" of the universe (what was more extraordinary here was perhaps that the average person never reflected, unless solipsistically, about such matters at all), but thought of himself, with a saving Highland Cynicism, as a single factor whose conduct vitally affected it."[2]

Jacqueline has a high regard for her adopted father when she says "oh, it's all holy enough in its way, all too holy... Daddy's had the idea that people like him are needed to combat the evil side of it all, which he maintains is flourishing now more than *it did* in the Middle Ages. He's got a bee in his bonnet about Hitler, for example."[3] Mc Candless is not to be written off as a white magician dabbling in the esoteric cult of Cabbala without any bearing on the compelling concerns of life. Mc Candless's concern with spiritualists is different from that of clairvoyants or seers running their consulting rooms and clinics at Nanaimo. The street of calculators of nativities and dreamers of dream in the street of Nanaimo has something commercial about it in the manner of Madame Sosostris in T.S. Eliot's *The Wasteland.* Mc Candless's concern for spiritual values is for redeeming the civilization that has fallen a prey to sordid materialism. The fortune-tellers of Nanaimo are a pretentious lot intent on making money by practising deception on people as cheats and impostors do in Ben Jonson's world.

Ethan makes a mockery of these charlatans having a mushroom growth at Nanaimo: "Of these fortune-tellers Ethan speaks jestingly, ...it was a pity the cards were not more consonant with the signs, that neither Friar Bacon's brazen head, nor the sign of Mother Shipton, nor yet that of Merlin himself were in evidence, something that would have combined the signboard idea with a more accurate evocation than that provided by Ye Coach and Horses of what was to be found within, and would have been, besides, more historically

1. *Ibid.*, pp. 10-11.
2. *Ibid.*, p. 31.
3. *Ibid.*, p. 30.

consistent...Madame Zog, Famed Albanian Seer, in this tea shop, 1-3, 4-7 daily, Teacup readings or crystal."[1]

Draco the Druid Diviner is one of the fortune-tellers and it is a travesty of his trade that he says to Jacqueline that he half-believes in his trade. Draco feels that the trade of prognostication is not a flourishing one, unless it is scientific and this intrusion of science into the realm of spirit runs counter to Mc Candless's belief in the holy supernatural and Ethan's fleeting intimations of the mysterious order watching the affairs of man.

To a casual reader *October Ferry to Gabriola* appears to be deficient in character-creation and Malcolm Lowry's observation in one of his letters to Albert Erskine also lends support to the thesis that the novel is lacking in character-creation in traditional sense. But a sensitive engagement with the text reveals that Malcolm Lowry has the capacity for creating characters with their separate identities and has the power to make subtle discriminations amongst them. The spirituality of Angus Mc Candless is different from the pretension to the spirituality of the fortune-tellers of Nanaimo and the visionary gleams, that at moments, illumining the guilt-ridden psyche of Ethan, make fortune-tellers a band of impostors and Ethan's visionary gleams have also a richer timbre than that of his father-in-law, Mc Candless.

It is this visionary gleam that comes to the rescue of Ethan and Jacqueline, when they are stricken with despair on their eviction from the primal bliss of Eridanus. Malcolm Lowry has such a profound insight into the abyss that opens up in the soul of a man, when he is in the grip of vile passions. He portrays the recess of the heart of his two principal characters, Ethan and Jacqueline, in their moments of illumination as well as in the moments of disillumination. The phase of disillumination reaches, when Ethan and Jacqueline drift apart, the former dragging the latter into the labyrinth of expiation of his guilt and the latter resisting to be drawn into the maze spun by the former.

1. *Ibid.*, pp. 239-40.

They are in an impasse and this impasse is overcome when the second phase in their lives begins, the phase that launches them into a meaningful life. The Catholic priest of Gabriola acts as a catalyst setting off a change for the better in the life of Ethan and Jacqueline. It is a great irony of Ethan's life that he, who had acquitted himself well in a shipwreck on lake Ontario, who had saved a young couple for drawning in the Niagara River and who had shown courage in dealing with hazards in course of living at Eridanus, is in the grip of despair. Ethan, The Watcher on the Threshold, a prey to appalling desperation implores the Catholic priest to make a prayer for his soul.

In the benign presence of the priest Ethan undergoes a change, when he experiences horror being followed and "almost obliterated by the inerrarable sense of the miraculous."[1] The loving ministration of the Catholic priest is the harbinger of a new life for Ethan. In Ethan self-introspection begins with a new vigour impelling him to make a burial of his old self obsessed with guilt and hatred and work out a new life style based on love and trust. Malcolm Lowry very sensitively portrays this evolution of Ethan from a soul sick to death to a soul buoyed up by the new bracing breeze of life: "Far from a decent magnanimous fellow he was becoming as a husband a monstrosity of selfishness, childishness, and self-pity. And on top of that he spoiled everything with his flippancy. Did he cherish Jacqueline as tenderly as Mr. Neiman so obviously cherished his wife? Alas, that had perhaps occurred to Jacqueline too... He was sick. Self-sacrifice! The priest was right. He would sacrifice himself for his wife, starting at this instant."[2]

Ethan's separation from the sacred mysteries of life releases in him an abstract passion of hatred, so all-consuming and so utterly implacable, that it feels like an invasion from the fearful wrath that was sweeping the world but the priests' paternal reassurance makes him conscious of a beneficent spirit working in the interest of man. Keeping in abeyance the

1. *Ibid* , p. 304.
2. *Ibid.*, pp. 315-16.

sceptic in him Ethan speaks of the ubiquitous good spirit with humility and awe: "Like light, but quicker than light, this spirit must be, and able to be in a thousand places at once in a thousand disguises, most of them, as befits our intelligence, absurd, this spirit that terrifies without terror, but that endeavours, above all to communicate, to say no more than perhaps, 'Hold on, I am here'."[1]

The presence of the priest marks a shift in Ethan's attitude. Of this change in Ethan Richard K. Cross rightly avers "He is not ready to undertake a grand leap of faith, yet the rekindling of religious hope serves to buoy him up."[2] With this stirring of a new life in him Ethan embarks on a journey to Gabriola by ferry from Nanaimo. This resolve of Ethan to go to Gabriola in the face of all odds speaks of the sterner stuff that he exhibits in himself. Jacqueline wants to take a softer course by returning to Eridanus but Ethan thinks of the undesirability of that course. Ethan, who has seen so much of heart break and despair, that it is not in the lot of man to taste the felicity of paradise for good, as it is not destined for Thomas Mann's *Hans Castorp* to remain forever in the Berghof, Ethan too has to leave Eridanus and confront his destiny, if he has to attain equilibrium.

(C) TECHNIQUE

Mrs. Lowry's observations in respect of depth of *Under the Valcano* apply even more strongly to Malcolm Lowry's formal organization in his later works, especially *October Ferry to Gabriola*: "His astonishing awareness of the thickness of life, of the layers, the depths, of the abysses, interlocking and interrelated, causes him to write a symphony where anyone else would have written a sonata or at most a concerto, and this makes his work sometimes appear dispersed, whereas actually the form and context have arisen so inextricably one from the other that they cannot be dissociated."[3] This rich

1. *Ibid.*, p. 320
2. K. Cross, Richard: *Malcolm Lowry*, p. 82.
3. Lowry, Malcolm: *Selected Letters*, p. 421.

formal organization has been effected by a couple of devices such as the streams-of-consciousness, the flashback and the musicalization of the structure of the novel.

The technique of stream-of-consciousness, which has been Malcolm Lowry's forte all through his novels, imparts a rich texture to the novel. Malcolm Lowry takes recourse to this technique, because he finds it capacious enough to accommodate the belief of Ethan, the protagonist of *October Ferry to Gabriola*, that "man is constantly in flux and constantly changing."[1] The separate selves of Ethan jostling with one another in his mind find an evocative portrayal, when Ethan broods over the toy model of Moscow he receives from his father: "...lifting it whole out of a mysterious deep-Christmas smelling wooden box, a beautiful toy model of Moscow, a city of tiny magical gold domes, pumpkin—or Christmas-bell-shaped, sparkle with Christmas tinsel-scented snow, bright as new silver half-crowns, and of minuscule Byzantine chimes; and at whose miniature frozen street corners waited minute sleighs, in which Ethan had imagined years later lilliputian Tchitchikovs brooding, or corners where lurked snow bound Raskolnikovs, their hands stayed from murder evermore: much later still he was to become unsure whether the city, sprouting with snow-freaked onions after all, was intended to be Moscow or St. Petersburg, for part of it seemed in memory built on little piles in the "water", like Eridanus; the city coming out of the box he was certain was magic too—for he had never seen it again after that evening of his father's return, in a strange astrakhan—collared coat and Russian fur cap—the box that was always to be associated also with his mother's death, which had occurred shortly therefter, the magic bulbar city going back into the magic scented box forever, and himself too afraid of his father to ask him about it later—though how beautiful for years to him was the word "city", the carilloning word "city" in the Christmas hymn, "Once in Royal David's City", and the tumultuous angel-winged city that was Bunyan's celestial city; beautiful, that was, until he "saw" a

1. Lowry, Malcolm: *October Ferry to Gabriola*, p. 61.

city—it was London—for the first time, sullen, in fog, and bloodshot as if with the fires of hell...".[1]

This passage makes an interweaving of diverse motifs with remarkable psychological depth and stylistic richness. The first is the motif of the jollity and mirth of boyhood Ethan experiences on receiving the Christmas gift from his father, the second is the motif of guilt brewing in the psyche of Raskolnikov in Dostoevsky's *Crime and Punishment*, the third is the motif of callousness of Ethan's father in taking the gift away from his young son, the fourth is the motif of fear with which Ethan cowers at the very idea of an indifferent father, the fifth is the motif of sadness arising from the depth of his mother, the sixth is the motif of Eridanus, the cherished land of happiness, the seventh is the motif of spiritual elation engendered by the allusion to David's City in Christian hymns and to celestial city of Bunyan and finally the motif of the sullen city of London enveloped in fog recalling to mind T.S. Eliot's Unreal City of London folded in the blanket of fog in *The Waste Land* and giving a foretaste of damnation that is round the corner.

The mingling of all these motifs forms a microcosm of the novel reflecting the principal themes of damnation and salvation in the novel. A reader who is not responsive to the sure and unerring intermingling of a variety of experiences into a unity may charge Malcolm Lowry's *October Ferry to Gabriola* with breaking up into a swarm of unrelated impressions. It is a fact that the technique of stream-of-consciousness exceeds every other in its risk of terrible fluidity and its natural threat to balance, proportion and composure. As James Joyce tries to save himself from the danger of alarming diffuseness and uncritical subjectivity by making an interrelation amongst varied experiences and by tethering them to a point which helps to create an illusion of order, Malcolm Lowry establishes correspondences and harmonies underlying the diversities of experiences. He is a sure-footed technician, because he knows how to discipline the interior monologue.

1. Lowry, Malcolm: *October Ferry to Gabriola*, p. 8.

The meditations of Ethan compare well to the meditations of *To The Light House* or *Mrs. Dalloway*, whose heroines move towards infinity, when they are engaged in doing the domestic chores of mending the clothes and cooking the dinner or the rich flood of associations making the rich fabric of Joyce's Stephen or of Ana Livia's ebbing consciousness at the close of *Finnegans Wake*. Malcolm Lowry is not Dorothy Richardson in whose novels the technique of stream-of-consciousness is vitiated by a lack of balance and proportion. It speaks well of the artistic scrupulousness of Malcolm Lowry that of the very outset of the novel, that is in Chapter Two I have just alluded to, the succeeds in encompassing in one breath the major themes he is going to develop in the novel in one breath.

The technique of flashback Malcolm Lowry uses in *October Ferry to Gabriola* adds to the rich formal organization of the novel. The first flashback recalls to mind the two films Ethan witnesses in the novel. The first is the film *Outward Bound* and the second is *Ins't ife Wonderful*? The first film *Outward Bound* Ethan sees at a suburban Toronto cinema is the film, when he is wooing Jacqueline. There is a great dichotomy between the amorous mood of courtship and the sinister and macabre film *Outward Bound.* The film *Outward Bound* is connected with suicide and the punishment for those who commit suicide. Persons committing suicide commute eternally on the spectral ferry between the earth and unbeholden land. This film gives a premonition of the shape of things to come in the novel. The suicide of Peter Cordwainer, which fills Ethan with remorse, because Ethan has a feeling that he has goaded his friend Peter Cordwainer to commit suicide. The Gabriola Ferry, a nameless boat, painted a sinister yellow, is perhaps the ferry plying between the outer and inner world. The second film *Isn't Life Wonderful*?, a tale of immense suffering and eviction, Ethan sees just before he is betrothed to Jacqueline. This film holds the forebodings of the future of Ethan and Jacqueline. It is suggestive of the struggle of the two searching for happiness.

The se flashback relates to the film *The Wandering Jew*. This film is about someone who wants to die by fire and when he plunges into fire, the fire receeds. This tortuous predicament of someone, who is denied death despite his intense longing for it, is the predicament of Ethan. Ethan prays to Lord for deliverance, he wants a burial of his old self, and he craves a new life of felicity but that life escapes him. This flashback is also concerned with the destruction by fire in 1946 of Ethan's ancestral bourne Barkerville at Niagra-on-the Lake. With the burning of the house of his nativity is also connected a comic-horrific series of fire supposedly the work of poltergeists. Ethan also sees the film *Wuthering Heights*. This film too built up the sinister and terrifying world of Heathcliff. The Heathcliff universe has a kinship with the harrowing world of Ethan. Thus films, with their tales of ordeals and death, psychologically prepare the reader for the right type of responses he has to make, when he reads *October Ferry to Gabriola*.

The scene of the room in Ixion College at the University of Ely, where Peter Cordwainer commits suicide, is the last flashback. This flashback becomes a settled effect in the mind of Ethan and it is evoked by the advertisement of Mother Kettle—Simmered Soup. This advertisement is like an octopus that has fastened its tentacles on the mind of Ethan.

Malcolm Lowry's technique at places in *October Ferry to Gabriola* becomes Proustian in character. Speaking of the technique of Proust, especially Proust's mode of rendering time in his novels, E.M. Forster admires the ingenuity of Proust in altering the hands of the clock of time in his novels "so that his hero was at the same time period entertaining a mistress to supper and playing ball with his nurse in the park."[1] This technique that works through dislocation of time-sequence is designed for the unfolding of the past.

The memories and desires lying buried in the wallet of the past come out and invade the consciousness and in *October Ferry to Gabriola* a specimen of this swarming of the consciousness is evident when Ethan broods over his life after his ancestral house is burnt: "And, looking back, he seemed

1. Forster, E.M.: *Aspects of the Novel*, p. 37.

half to remember dreams forgotten at that time, dreams of guilt in which his father's loneliness in that house he had done so little to assuage and his own childhood loneliness was merged, dire dreams of infantile uprootings, and night journey across the sea, even imaginings of his own conception in the house, taking place now as a horrendous violation, now as an act of tenderest love; other dreams where his mother or grandmother seemed pleading with him, gently forgiving, impossibly to undo something already done; which, waking from them always with remorse and sorrow and helplessness on his soul, and always through some fading image of a house, appeared to him as though they must have somehow concerned their first home, and so led back in consciousness in those wool-gatherings of day which were more sinister, sometimes when driving alone to Toronto, or at moments of suspense or boredom in court, or of gaiety on another level, when helping Jacqueline wash dishes after a few drinks, led back in his mind to Peter Cordwainer again, the following out of some insane pattern of beginning retribution, though never to the understanding of it, or the complete desire to understand, or the sincere desire to forgive himself: or to seek help."[1]

This technique of moving through the corridors of time enables Ethan to vividly juxtapose so many memories, so many joys and desires of widely separated years and the distant period Ethan has lived through. This mingling of varied worlds within the brief compass of a passage just cited above is a method of evaluation of life by putting diverse segments of life together.

October Ferry to Gabriola, in the words of Malcolm Lowry himself, doesn't contain "one single conventional virtue of the normal story...".[2] The prime conventional virtue of the novel form is external action, 'plot' as we call it—and realised conflict between characters. In a Lowry novel the emphasis is not on external action. There is almost a surfeit of movement internally, movement within the psyche of a character. Tension

1. Lowry, Malcolm: *October Ferry to Gabriola*, p. 72.
2. Lowry, Malcolm: *Selected Letters*, p. 339.

within the mind of the protagonist is so compelling that it renders any other conflict superfluous. In the preface to *Dark as the Grave wherein My Friend is Laid* Douglas Day rightly observes: "What sustains all his work is not plot, nor dialogue nor movement, but the spinning up and down which is amazing in all the senses of the word. The pace of this mind is such that it generates great tension and excitement, so that the 'plot' of a Lowry novel is the movement of the mind of the author—or, shall we say the mind of the protagonist."[1]

In *October Ferry to Gabriola* Ethan is seen moving through the grooves of the mind and weaving a dense texture. In one of his unpublished letter Malcolm Lowry says that *October Ferry to Gabriola* is "not intended to fall into any particular category or obey any of the normal rules of the novel."[2] It is a fact that *October Ferry to Gabriola* does not observe novelistic conventions of plot and characterisation in the traditional manner. Its form is such that it is nearer the composition of a symphony, not a sonata or concerto. In a sonata or concerto movements are few but a symphony is the culmination of diverse movements into a unity. Speaking of this symphonic form in novel, Aldous Huxley in *Point Counter Point* observes that the musicalization of fiction consists in the construction of a novel in which there are changes of moods and abrupt transitions but all modulations not merely from one key to another, but from mood to mood is developed into a unity.

In *October Ferry to Gabriola* there is an orchestration of various moods of Ethan. The various facets of the mind of Ethan—rational, political, ironic or obsessive and anguished, fantastic and manic—are unified into a whole. In *October Ferry to Gabriola* feelings are blended in a complex manner from the realistic to the fantastic. Like a Xylophone player Ethan plays on the different keys and makes modulations from one key to the other and this perpetual shifting of moods and their development into a unity is very much near the symphonic form.

1. Day, Douglas: Preface to *Dark as the Grave wherein My Friend is Laid*, p. 8.
2. Quoted by Richard K. Cross in Malcolm Lowry a preface to his Fiction, p. 76.

Ethan's changing moods mirroring the various movements of a symphony is summed up here: "Mightn't be equally well consider that he'd been vouchsafed, was so being vouchsafed, a glimpse into the very workings of creation itself?—indeed with this cognition Ethan seemed to see before his eyes whole universes eternally condensing and recondensing themselves out of the "immaterial" into the "material", and as the continued visualization of their Creator, being radiated back again. While meantime here on earth the "material" was only cognizable through the mind of man! What was real, what imaginary? Yes, but couldn't the meaning, the message, for them, be simply that there had been a message at all? Yes, could he not just as well tell himself, as Cyprian of Antioch, that here God had beaten the devil at his own game, that magic was checkmated by miracle!"[1]

As the Marx hymn weaves stories in the collection titled *Hear Us O Lord From Heaven Thy Dwelling Place* into a unity, the song Ethan whistles "what of the night, watchman, what of the night?" and Hooray the harbour is near! Lo, the red Light!... Christians cast anchor now, Heaven is thy home!"[2] is the underlying music that binds the diversity of materials in *October Ferry to Gabriola* into a wholeness. This underlying music also confirms the musicalization of the structure.

One of the modes of organizing novels to which Malcolm Lowry often feels drawn, is Conradian in character. In his later phase we find Conrad going to his early works and absorbing themes and ideas from them. In his tales *Chance* and *Victory* Conrad returns to the world of his early stories, picks up materials there and transmutes them into something new with new ambiguities and depths. In *October Ferry to Gabriola* we find Malcolm Lowry returning to his early works such as *Hear Us O Lord From Heaven Thy Dwelling Place* and to *Under the Volcano* for the sake of assimilating ideas from them and transforming those ideas with a new perception.

The inferno of *Under the Volcano* reappears in *October Ferry to Gabriola* and the novel becomes the most "Satanically

1. Lowry, Malcolm: *October Ferry to Gabriola*, pp. 147-48.
2. *Ibid*, p. 246.

horrendous document",[1] as Malcolm Lowry himself acknowledges in his letter to Albert Erskine. The Eridanus theme that occurs in the story *The Forest Path to the Spring* reappears in *October Ferry to Gabriola* with a new emphasis. Thus one of the techniques employed by Malcolm Lowry in *October Ferry to Gabriola* is in the manner of later Conrad in the sense that each book cumulates and absorbs the previous books. It appears as if Malcolm Lowry is doing a random mixing of overlapping versions but the truth is that he is engaged in discovering the hitherto unexploded possibilities in experiences.

Symbolic presentment of the theme is also a device favourite with Malcolm Lowry. But he himself points out the flaw in his symbolic presentment in *October Ferry to Gabriola*: "... symbols are pointed at blatantly instead of being concealed or subsumed in the material, or better still simply not there at all, it is—or is as it stands—repetitions to the point beyond that which you can believe."[2] The slow, stealthy, despairing deepening of his mind finds its symbolic enactment in the swirling tides of Eridanus: "It was as though he had been watching, on a dark still day, one of those immense black afternoon tides of autumn slowly brimming up beneath the windows: and now were trying not to watch it, on the same day grown gradually a blustery turbulent one of southeast wind and murk and rain, with the branches murderously crashing down in the forest behind the cabin; one of those tides that rose ever higher as they approached, say, the October full moon, that full moon which was tonight, he remembered, the tide already beginning to come in now too in the gulf below them to their right, the invisible tide in the invisible gulf, that same tide they must battle or whose ebbing treacheries would carry them perhaps, this afternoon, one way or another, on their ferry to Gabriola; yes, and now not so much brimming as lashing and driving up beneath their windows, and with a venomous roaring, devouring, grinding sibilance: it wasn't that the house was endangered by tidewater, for all the cabins were built just to

1. Lowry, Malcolm: *Selected Letters*, p. 339.
2. *Ibid.*, p. 339.

surmount the highest tide, and only once had it happened apparently, when an onshore gale blowing for days and heavy rain had obstructed the normal ebb, that some of the cabins were flooded; but that these tides at their highest might dislodge and set afloat one or other of the huge timbers, left stranded all summer on the beach by the previous spring or winter tides, great writhing snags of roots,...".[1]

Though this symbolic projection of the mind of Ethan passing through a phase of agony is overelaborate, it is apt in the sense that it vividly recreates the lashing waves dashing against Ethan's cabin and generating in him the feeling of impending doom. It also goes to the credit of Malcolm Lowry, that with great lyrical power and profusion of images, he creates unforgettable pictures of life in the midst of darkness that sometimes threatens to overwhelm Ethan. It is the gift of imagery and lyricism that gives *October Ferry to Gabriola* a character somewhat absent from his earlier works.

The imperishable impulse to life Ethan and Jacqueline discover is beautifully rendered here: "the golden robin that was the Baltimore oriole and knot expert, and master builder, at its complex work of nesting, whistling in its rich contralto; they had seen the two orioles making their nest together earlier in the afternoon, the Llewelyns themselves the watchers on the threshold, watching them weaving happily their wonderful nest of fibres and plant down and hairs and string (rebuild, we shall rebuild), the female thrusting a fibre into the nest and then, this was the wonderful part, reaching over to the inside and pulling the string through with her little beak, tugging with all her night to make everything all "a'taunto", solid and tight,...".[2] Another poetic image of vibrant life against the menacing backdrop is the example of Lowry's love of life through his protagonist Ethan in *October Ferry to Gabriola*: "...and the ecstasies of bobolinks twittering and bobolinking in the blue, bobbling on the links, or bringing rushes of rollicking song downwind, like imagined tintinnabulating herebells, like tinkling bluebells, darting over the "moat" of the old

1. Lowry, Malcolm: *October Ferry to Gabriola*, pp. 76-77.
2. *Ibid.*, p. 111.

fort—the bastion now the out-of-bounds at the short fourth: "Ein Festerburg ist unser Gott." Ethan said (observing at this moment that the old Noronic—"Bask in the warm breezes of Ontario on the boat deck of Canada's favourite pleasure boat"—was halfway to Toronto) and where, among what appeared cunning contracallations, they found an antique long-lost golf ball of forgotten make named the "Zodiak Zone"; the blithe bobolink, friend of hay and clover, the merry bobolink that was also called (ex post factor knowledge too) skunk blackbird, le goglu, Dolichonyx oryzivorous; the bobolink that said clink."[1]

The alliteration in "bobolinks twittering and bobolinking in the blue, bobbling on the links", "rushes of rollicking", "the blithe bobolink", artisticaily evoke the bouncing song bird chanting mellifluous songs. Lowry's love of life expressed through Jacqueline's enormous fascination for flowers of various hues blooming in plenty at Niagra-on-the-Lake, the loveliest town of Canada: "...that eastern spring, every bit as extravagant as the tamarind mulberry and fire-colored autumns, and coming with such a rush and bloom of life after the breaking up of the ice on the lake; the fountainous elm trees with their pale green fluttering leaves overarching the stately avenues of the deserted town (which a few weeks hence would be as crowded each weekend with tourists from Toronto and across the border as a Coney Island beach) and the blue lake itself beyond; the white dogwood, the pink dogwood, the celestial clouds of peach blossom, the capricious cardinals so splendidly crested and caparisoned in scarlet (so red, she had written, that when they flash through the trees you don't believe it), the trapezing scarlet tanagers that lived in their orchard, so precariously in a nest of leaves on the end of a branch; the first snowdrops and crocus in her garden; and the fantastic cause—wood tree; a flurry of snow out of a clear sky...".[2]

1. *Ibid.*, p. 113.
2. *Ibid.*, pp. 87-88.

Conclusion

Stephen Spender in his book *The Struggle of the Modern* observes that all through twentieth century literature there have been two kinds of writers. On the one hand there are those who have no artistic pretensions and engage in a direct prosaic way with the social and political realities of life. If they register a protest against the social and political ethos, they do so with some degree of revolutionary optimism. They believe that through their ideas there is a possibility of social and moral regeneration and literature becomes a tool for effecting the desired change. To Spender writers of this group are called contemporaries and he includes among them such writers as Shaw, Wells, Bennett and Orwell.

But there are those who are sceptical of the approach of writers Stephen Spender labels 'contemporaries'. They have a distrust of the pragmatic approach to life discernible in the writings of contemporaries. They seek a radical transformation of conventional forms of communication. The new idiom they seek to devise will articulate poetically the inner crisis of sensibility, a crisis which often manifests itself in the search for a tradition which has been lost or broken. They are moderns such as James Joyce, Virginia Woolf and T.S. Eliot. They are inaugurators of modern aesthetics. Though Stephen Spender's distinction between the modern and the contemporary is open to qualification but it is a useful one. The modernist movement in fiction begins with the last decade of the nineteenth century and continues till the first two decades of the twentieth century. Flaubert, Conrad and James Joyce are proponents of the new theory of novel. All important modern novelists such as James, Conrad, Joyce and Virginia Woolf, write their best work by 1924 and are also dead by then. Since the death of major modern novelists just alluded to, the unremitting concern for form, which is their credo, is on the wane and peters out in the thirties.

In the thirties there is a swing to the social content of the novel as practised in the novels of contemporaries such as Evelyn Waugh and C.P. Snow. Chronologically, Malcolm Lowry belongs to the category of the 'contemporaries' because he is a post-war novelist. But his novels do not exhibit social realism observable in other contemporary writers. He appears to be a novelist outside the mainstream of novels written in the thirties. There are two other novelists of significance who stay out of the mainstream of English novel in the post-war decade and they are Lawrence Durrell and Samuel Beckett. These three writers—Lawrence Durrell, Samuel Beckett and Malcolm Lowry—do not fit in with the conventional account of the development of the post-war English novel as a movement from pre-war experimentalism to post-war realism.

They are writers displaced from the English sequence, yet, they stand in oblique yet significant relation to contemporary English writing. Though they are not similar writers, but they agree on the point that the social novel has no appeal for them. In a period when provincialism and localism are in the ascendency in English writing, they make their lives and find many of their artistic sources and influences elsewhere. They deliberately seek displacement from the mainstream of contemporary English novel and are obsessively concerned with an experimental and cosmopolitan view of art. They are unhoused and expatriates, because they subject themselves to an international range of influence and "take technical expertise and ostentation as an epistemological imperative in art and all stake large part of their artistic effort on procuring the right conditions, economic and contextual, for maintaining an ethos of artistic dedication. They have their links with great modernists of the previous two or three decades."[1] Durrell and Beckett seek inspiration from Paris, the centre of avant-garde artists but Lowry's artistic centres are Cambridge, Paris and New York.

Thus, instead of being insular Malcolm Lowry exposes himself to new movements and fashions in literary thought. A reading of his novels provides us with sufficient evidence of his continuity with the great modernists of the first two decades of the twentieth century obserable in the texture of deep literary allusiveness, the commitment to formal experiment, the quality of strain and anguish typical of the modern age. His commitment and dedication to artistic shaping and organisation of his material is serious and unflinching. Malcolm Bradbury rightly says, "He shows the dedication of a man of great intelligence and critical instinct attempting a full and responsible achievement."[2] His commitment to form is borne out by the recurrence of the phrase 'design governing postures' in his letters. By 'design governing postures' he means his rigorous concern for form, a serious quest for a design in the heterogeneous chaotic facts of life.

He feels the imperious need of form, because he knows that the origins of his novels lie deep in the realm of the irrational. The promptings of the irrational are shapeless and a novelist, who makes a descent into the irrational, cannot make what he discovers in the abyss, orderly and meaningful, unless he is possessed of a sense of form. In the terminology of Jung, Malcolm Lowry belongs to the category of writers called 'Visionary' and not to the category of writers called 'Psychological'. Contemporary novelists such as Evelyn Waugh and C.P. Snow concerned with the social reality will be treated 'Psychological' writers. Psychological writers in Jungian aesthetics are not writers of the stream-of-consciousness. They are writers who derive their "material and method from the sphere of conscious human experience—from the psychic foreground of life."[3]

1. Bradbury Malcolm: *Possibilities*, p. 181.
2. *Ibid.*, p. 82.
3. Quoted in Douglas Day's *Malcolm Lowry: A Biography*, p. 467.

They are conscious and reason-oriented writers but Malcolm Lowry is a writer who shows concern for a "primordial experience which surpasses man's understanding and to which in his weakness he may easily succumb."[1] He is concerned with experiences "arising from timeless depths; glamorous, daemonic, grotesque, it bursts as under our human standards of value and aesthetic form, a terrifying tangle of eternal chaos...."[2] A novelist like Malcolm Lowry dealing with the terrifying tangle of eternal chaos must have a sense of order and form, if he wants a comprehension of his themes in the novel by the common reader. Malcolm Lowry's *Under the Volcano* is about diabolical powers in man that terrify him. First, Malcolm Lowry moves into the terrifying tangle of chaos in the mind of Geoffrey, the British Consul and then travels back into consciousness where he finds the organising ability that is necessary to give his vision a coherence.

He is a genius in the sense that he has dared to expose himself to the full impact of the vision of an educated and urban British Consul Geoffrey Firmin in the grip of infernal powers, and is still able to return to the world of consciousness to lend the most satisfying shape to that vision. He shows Geoffrey moving through landscapes of destruction and waste, landscapes of hell in which symbolic ruination abounds. It is the picture of a man who is equipped with the consequences of human action and yet able to make a self-destructive choice. We find such an archetype in Marlowe's Faustus who knowingly sells his soul to the agents of Satan.

In our times Graham Greene and Thomas Mann paint such pictures but Graham Greene's characters are perhaps too small and Thomas Mann's Adrian Leverkuhn seems driven more by disease than by free will but Malcolm Lowry produces a Faustean masterpiece. He is dying of drink and like any tragic hero, he is fully aware of the choice he has made. He clings to his sloth, he needs salvation through love but will not utter the words that will bring it. But in spite of his inexorable movement to damnation he becomes aware of the

1. *Ibid.*, p. 467.
2. *Ibid.*, p. 467.

supervening bond of life. This awareness of the supervening bond of life is the result of his consciousness of form when he separates Geoffrey from his personal self and places him in the context of values that are outside time. In *Ultramarine* too he develops a dialectic between exile and home in the character of Dana Hilliot and the novel is built out of the tension between the surroundings of home symbolised by Dana Hilliot's parents and his beloved Janet and a search for an identity through voyage.

In his novel *Lunar Caustic* the protagonist, Bill Plantagenet, in the manner of Geoffrey Firmin of *Under the Volcano*, makes a descent into the maelstrom, the foul core of his world. But the tone changes in *Lunar Caustic*, when Bill Plantagenet has the compelling urge to liberate himself from the tentacles of despair fastened on his soul, when he shows no sign of slackening his resolve to purge himself of guilt that impairs his hold on life. This pursuit of life-giving forces gets a shot in the arm, when Malcolm Lowry creates the character of Ethan Llewelyn, in *October Ferry to Gabriola* who, though dispossessed, plagued by fear and guilt, moves unrelentingly towards the numinous power transcending this world of ours. This supernatural power has the miraculous property healing the breach in the psyche of Ethan Llewelyn. It is not the testament of hope that gives it a mere optimistic ring in a black universe. It is a testament of hope resulting from coming to terms with the antinomies of life. Thus Malcolm Lowry shows the sign of a developing artist who initially fumbles for an identity but discovers an identity of his own after having wrestled with life in all its immedicable horror of opposites.

Bibliography

I. Published Works of Malcolm Lowry

The following are arranged in chronological order.

Ultramarine, London: Jonathan Cape, 1933. Revised edition, with introductory note by Margerie Bonner Lowry, Jonathan Cape, London. 1962.*

Under the Volcano, London: Jonathan Cape, 1947. (With a preface by Stephen Spender). Reprinted in 1970.*

Hear Us O Lord From Heaven Thy Dwelling Place, First Published in the USA, 1961. Penguin Books, 1969.*

Selected Poems, San Francisco: City Lights Books, 1962. Edited by Earle Birnly with the assistance of Margerie Bonner Lowry.

Lunar Caustic, First published in the Paris Review, No. 29, 1963. Penguin Books, 1969.*

Selected Letters, Capricorn Books Edition, 1969.*

Dark as the Grave Wherein My Friend Is Laid, First Published by Jonathan Cape 1969. Penguin Books, 1972.*

October Ferry to Gabriola, New York: World 1970. Edited by Margerie Lowry. First Plume Printing, 1971.*

N.B. I have made references to the Publications of Malcolm Lowry with asterisk marks in the manner shown above.

II. Selected Works Concerning Malcolm Lowry

The following are arranged in alphabetical order.

Allen, Walter, *Tradition and Dream*. Published in Penguin Books, 1965.

Bradbury, Malcolm and Palmer, David. *The Contemporary English Novel*, Edward Arnold (Publishers) Ltd., 1979.

Bradbrook, M.C., *Malcolm Lowry : His Art and Early Life*, Cambridge University Press, 1974.

Burgess, Anthony, "Europe's Day of the Dead", *Spectator*, 20 (January 1967), 74.

Burgess, Anthony, *The Novel Now*, Faber and Faber, 24 Russell Square London, 1967.

Day, Douglas, *Malcolm Lowry : A Biography*, London, Oxford Univesity Press, 1974.

Dodson B. Daniel, *Malcolm Lowry*, Columbia University Press, New York and London, 1970.

Heilman B. Robert, "Four Novels", *The Sewance Review*, Vol. LV, 1947.

Markson, David, "Malcolm Lowry: A Reminiscence", *Nation*. CCII, 16 (February 7, 1966), 164-67.

Smith, Anne, *The Art of Malcolm Lowry*, Vision Press Limited, London, 1978.

Spender, Stephen, "Introduction to Under the Volcano", Jonathan Cape. Thirty Bedford Square, London, 1967.

Stern, James, "Malcolm Lowry: A First Impression", *Encounter*, XXIX 3 (September 1967), 58-68.

III. Selected Works Concerning the Art of Fiction

Allott, Miriam, *Novelists on the Novel*, London, Routledge and Kegan Paul Ltd., 1959.

Bergonzi, Bernard, *The Situation of the Novel*, Published in Pelican Books, 1972.

Booth C. Wayne, *The Rhetoric of Fiction*, The University of Chicago Press, 1961.

Calderwood L. James and Toliver E. Harold, *Perspectives on Fiction*, New York, Oxford University Press, 1968.

Forster, E.M., *Aspects of the Novel*. Penguin Books Ltd., 1962.

Harvey, W.J., *Character and the Novel*, Cornell University Press, 1965.

James, Henry, *The House of Fiction*, London, Rupert Hart-Davis, 1957.

Karl R. Fredrick, *A Reader's Guide to the Contemporary English Novel,* Thames and Hudson London, 1963.

Leavis, Q.D., *Fiction and the Reading Public,* London, 1934.

Liddell, Robert, *A Treatise on the Novel,* Jonathan Cape, 1947.

Lodge, David, *Language of Fiction,* Routledge and Kegan Paul, London, 1966.

Lubbock, Percy, *The Craft of Fiction,* London, 1921.

Schorer, Mark, "Technique as Discovery", Hudson Review, 1 (Spring, 1948), 67-68.

IV. Selected Works Concerning Modern Aesthetics and Some Secondary Sources

Jung, C.G., *The Spirit in Man, Art and Literature,* Collected Works, Vol. XV, New York, 1966.

Read, Herbert, *Art Now,* Faber and Faber Limited, 1960.

Read, Herbert, *The Philosophy of Modern Art,* 1963.

Lawrence, D.H., *Studies in Classic American Literature,* The Phenix Edition, Heinemann, London, 1964.

Wilson, Edmund, *Axel's Castle,* The Fontana Library, 1961.

Jung, C.G., *Modern Man in Search of a Soul,* Routledge and Kegan Paul Ltd., London, E.C. 4, 1961.

N.B. References to the Publications of critical books on Malcolm Lowry and other secondary materials relating to his novels have been given in a consolidated form from Sections II to IV of the Bibliography.

Index